To Margaret and Brian,

with Very Best Wishes

Graham Crosbie

9. 8. 2010

A Country Cook's Garden in South West Scotland

by Susan Crosthwaite

*This book is dedicated to my husband Robin,
children Duncan and Fiona and parents
Dennis and Olga Tinsley.*

Published by S.Crosthwaite © 2002
www.cossescountryhouse.com

ISBN: 0-9544179-0-9

Designed & Printed by Stranraer and Wigtownshire Free Press.

CONTENTS
Introduction

5.	May	Watercolour print "Dogs in the Bluebell Woods

           Gardens: Glenwhan at Dunragit.
                           Broughton House at Kirkcudbright.
                           Bargany Gardens and the Kennedy/Dalrymple-Hamilton History.

Menu

Caesar Salad
Fresh Halibut with Sorrel Sauce garnished with Mousseline of
Spinach, Pommes de Terre Forestière. Broad Beans
Brandy Snap Cones filled with Rhubarb Fool served with Rhubarb and
Ginger Sauce
Scottish Cheese and Home-made Oatcakes

6.	June	Watercolour print "Azaleas"

Castle Kennedy Gardens and its history
Salmon Fishing

Menu

Fresh Asparagus with a light Butter Sauce
Local Salmon baked with Lime and Green Peppercorns served with
Gooseberry and Dill Cream
New Ayrshire Epicure Potatoes, Mange Tout, Broccoli
Strawberry Shortcake with Strawberry and Elderflower Sauce
Scottish Cheese and Home-made Oatcakes

7.	July	Watercolour print "Cosses Country House and Garden"

History of the Kennedies and Culzean castle

Menu

Courgettes stuffed with Tomatoes, Shallots and Peppers finished with
Mornay Sauce
Ballantrae Lobster with Cucumber and Strawberry Salad. Green
Mayonnaise, New Potatoes, Summer Vegetable Salad
Blackcurrant and Redcurrant Brûlée
Scottish Cheese and Home-made Oatcakes

8.	August	Water-colour print 'Cosses' "Hidden in a Valley"

Isle of Arran :
The geography of the Island
About the golf Courses
Brodick Castle
The Arran Distillery

The Isle of Cumbrie
The Ayrshire Flower Show

Menu

Ballantrae Prawns with Garlic, Spring Onions, Cream and Whisky
Guinea Fowl cooked on a mirepoix of Vegetables with Saffron and
Ginger finished with a Port and Berry Sauce
Platter of Cosses Summer Vegetables
Plum Tarte Tâtin with Home-made Ice Cream
Scottish Cheese and Home-made Oatcakes

9.	September	Watercolour print "Dusk falls on Newbridge in the centre of Ayr"

The Picts in Ayrshire :
Dalquharran and Kilkerran

William Wallace

Ayr: Racecourse
The Waverly
Theatres

Golf Courses in Southwest Scotland

Menu

Mushroom and Tobermory Cheddar Feuillete
Fillet of Beef, locally reared and cooked to taste, served with a Whisky
Cream Dijon Sauce.
Château Potatoes, Mixed Salad.
Baked Autumn Bliss Raspberry Creams
Scottish Cheese and Home-made Oatcakes

10. October   Watercolour print "Autumn in the Garden"

Walking in Southwest Scotland:
Southern Upland Way
Stinchar Falls and the Galloway Hills
Sraiton and Barr walks - the Carrick Hills
Girvan Walks
Sawney Bean's Cave
Walking in Ballantrae and it's local history
Glen App

Menu

Garden Herb Crêpes filled with Dunsyre Blue Cheese served with
Fresh Tomato Sauce
Monkfish Tails wrapped in Smoked Streaky Bacon with Garlic and
Thyme cream sauce
Smoked Salmon Risotto, Ribbon Cougettes
Apple and Blackberry Crumble with Creme Anglais
Scottish Cheese and Oatcakes

11. November   Watercolour print "Sunset"

Prehistoric man in Southwest Scotland
The Picts
Early Christianity
From the Picts to the Lords of Galloway to Robert the Bruce
The History of Galloway
The Covenanters

Menu

Filo Baskets with Courgettes, Onions, Peppers and Leeks with Mornay
Sauce surrounded by Fresh Tomato Sauce
Pork Fillet stuffed with Garlic and Herbs with a Cream Sauce.
Cauliflower and Romanesco Broccoli
Runner Beans tossed in Garlic. Mushroom and Potato Stacks
Hot Chocolate Soufflé
Scottish Cheese and Oatcakes

Acknowledgements

The creation of this book has been an exciting, interesting, enlightening experience and I would like to thank all those who have encouraged, helped and inspired me.

Liz Taylor for proof reading and editing some of my less than perfect use of the English language.
Pat and Struan Stevenson MEP for inspiration and the loan of their copy of the Carrick Gallovidian by J. Kevan McDouall F.S.A. Scot 1947., which is the source of much of the local history.
N. John F. Dalrymple Hamilton OBE.TD.DL and his wife **Sally-Anne** for the information about Bargany.
8th Marquis and 19th Earl Charles Kennedy and his wife **Ann**e for confirmation of the Kennedy History.
Davina, Countess of Stair for confirmation of Castle Kennedy History.
The Earl and Countess of Inchcape for confirmation of the Inchcape History.
Robert and Caroline Dalrymple's local knowledge.
Jeanette McCulloch's Ballantrae History and information from the library.
Sandra Pratt my art teacher.
Sponsors **Alexander Wines, Braehead Foods, Dalduff Farm Shop** and **J. Pieroni & Sons Ltd.**
Sam Miller, senior graphic designer and the team at Stranraer & Wigtownshire Free Press.

Mum and **Dad** who have encouraged me throughout.
And last, but always most, my husband **Robin** whose participation and computer skills have helped me enormously.

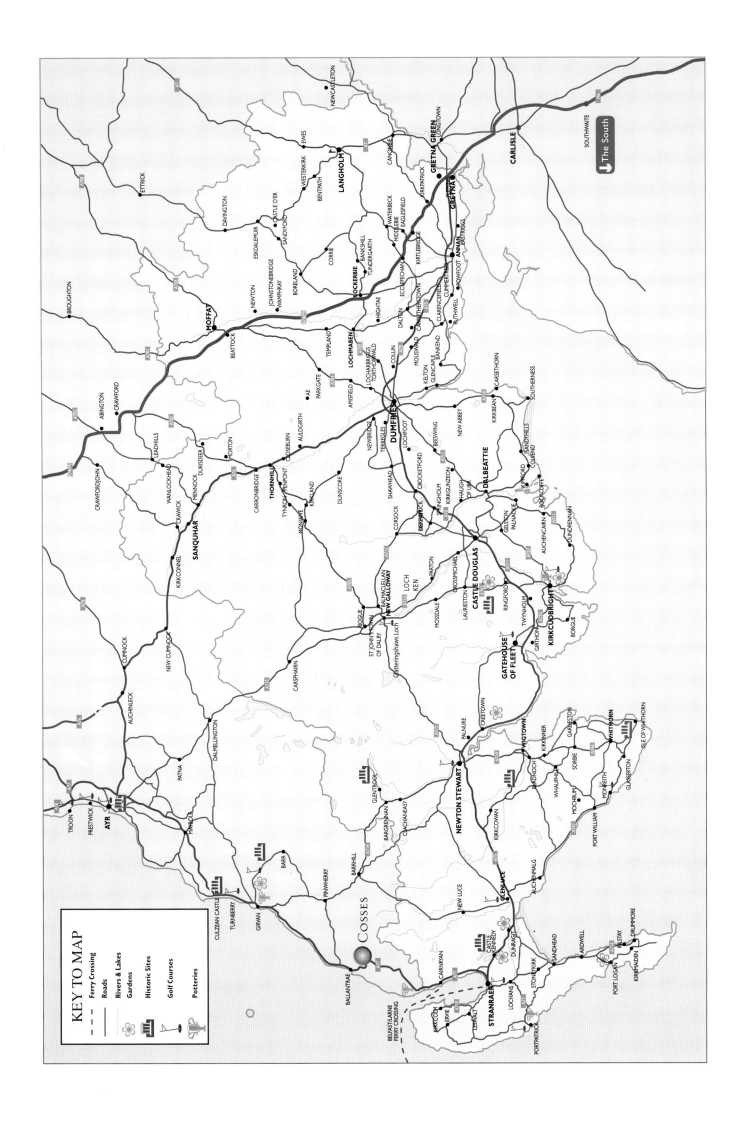

KEY TO MAP

Ferry Crossing
Roads
Rivers & Lakes
Gardens
Historic Sites
Golf Courses
Potteries

A COUNTRY COOK'S GARDEN IN SOUTHWEST SCOTLAND

Introduction

This is no ordinary book, but one inspired by the guests who have visited Cosses Country House, and experienced for themselves this "little bit of heaven" cosseted in the Ayrshire hills. The gastronomic delights produced in my country kitchen are all created from the best of Scottish produce, home grown vegetables, fruit and herbs from our own kitchen garden, locally reared beef, lamb, game, and freshly caught seafood.

The water-colour paintings, I hope, do justice to an area rich in natural beauty, and capture the ever changing mood and colours of the dramatic land and seascape that is Southwest Scotland. The information and anecdotes are designed to acquaint the reader with the colourful history, plentiful outdoor activities and natural resources.

Robin and I acquired this treasure on 29th July 1985. Since that time we have enjoyed sharing our passion for good food, wine and outdoor activities with our many guests. Friendly advice is always on hand to help make the most of your stay. Whether it be in the field of walking, cycling or merely motoring through the myriad of quiet roads, there is always something to see or do. The salmon rivers and trout lochs are well stocked, and even a moderately keen ornithologist would think he had found paradise. The abbeys, castles and standing stones mark the passage of time both turbulent and peaceful. Our rich soil and gentle temperate climate create the ideal environment for productive farming and the fabulous gardens for which South West Scotland is famous.

My recipes reflect the fact that all the preparation is completed by myself, therefore within the capabilities of any enthusiastic cook — a team of sous chefs is surplus to requirements!!

January

Snowdrops

(Watercolour)
Susan Crosthwaite

Menu:

Smoked Haddock Soufflé
Melba Toast
Gressingham Duckling Breast
with Czar Plum Sauce
Clapshot and Brussel Sprouts
Roast Vegetables
Flambéd Crêpes with Pineapple,
Banana and Grapes
Scottish Cheese and Homemade Oatcakes

January

Cosses, hidden in a valley on Crailoch Burn, a tributary of the famous River Stinchar, is the type of place we love to discover — a little bit of heaven— as described by many of our guests. Formerly part of the Ardstinchar estate, of which the first authentic reference to Ardstinchar Castle and its Barony, appears to have been about 1420. It is probable that Mary Macdouall brought the castle to her husband, John Kennedy de Dunure, as part of her wedding dowry, about 1340. The castle remained in the possession of the Bargany branch of the Kennedy clan and extended from the valley of the River Girvan to Carlock, 5 miles south of Ballantrae. The castle fell into disuse in the early part of the 18th century. (Many of the stones of the castle were used to build the Stinchar bridge).

The earliest records of Cosses itself indicate that it belonged to the Grahams of Knockdolian as a result of Helen , a daughter of Sir Thomas Kennedy of Bargany, bringing it to her marriage with John Grahame of Knockdolian in 1604. It was then a shooting lodge, sited at the ford where the road crosses Crailoch Burn. Blairquhan was acquired by James Kennedy in 1622 when he sold Culzean to his brother Alex and it was about this time when Cosses belonged to the Kennedies of Blairquhan. (Blairquhan was sold to Sir David Hunter Blair and between 1821 and 1824 a regency mansion was built - designed by William Burns. Today this is open to the public during August, and includes a walled garden and gallery devoted to the Scottish Colourists.)

In 1765 Cosses, as part of the Ardstinchar Estate was bought by John Allan of Kilphin. His daughter married the Rev. Donaldson and her son succeeded to the property. In 1916 the estate was bought by the Earl of Inchcape and Cosses became the home farm, where butter and cheese were made. By direction of the Right Hon. the Earl of Inchcape the fine agricultural and sporting estate of Auchairne was sold in 1950 and the Stewart family - the farming tenants - bought Cosses farm. With no male heir to continue farming, the Stewarts sold to our predecessors, the Cooksons, in 1963. The Cooksons did major renovations to the farmhouse, constructing the dining room and kitchen from the dairy, and creating the Iona Suite from a stable. In 1985 we bought the house with 12 acres (John and Rosemary Stevenson bought the remaining land to add to their farm - 'Meadowpark') and we have continued the renovations to the present day.

'Cosses', on some old maps is spelt as 'Corses, which means a hollow or groove, or a crossing - all of which pertain to 'Cosses', as it lies, hidden deep in the valley, at the crossing of 'Crailoch Burn'.

There isn't a season of the year that doesn't bring its own special magic to cherish at Cosses.
January is snowdrop time. They just appear like magic in the shrubbery and woodland, nodding their pretty heads, defying the winter winds, and calling out 'winter is waning'. This is a great time for bracing walks; a favourite of mine is in Culzean Country Park from the deer park through Happy Valley, round the Swan Pond, with it's snowdrops, along the cliffs and back to the castle - Bonzo, our black labrador, loves it too! Another favourite is the first section of the Southern Upland Way; parking at Kilantringan Lighthouse, at Blackhead (this is also the location of the best beach in the area on those hot summer days!). Walk along the cliffs, towards Portpatrick, often very breezy at this time of year; with spectacular cliff scenery and views along the coast and over to Ireland. Up and down through coves with steep steps, along rocky beaches, then up on the cliffs along the edge of Dunskey golf course and down all the steps into Portpatrick. Have a well deserved drink/lunch before retracing your steps - perhaps via Dunskey House.

Golf is also a great way to spend those crisp winter days. There is the champions choice of Turnberry (30 minutes from Cosses), Royal Troon, Old Prestwick (1 hour away) etc., or Dunskey, Stranraer, Girvan, Brunston (approximately half an hour away) just to name a few! The area offers an unlimited range of golfing opportunities and the mild weather allows most of the courses to be played throughout the year. Imagine a glorious winter's day, the sun shimmering off the sea , the birds singing overhead, you step onto the tee, the dew is sparkling on the fairway, you are ready to go — whack!— straight into the gorse (whins). Never mind, the great thing about golf is you always get a second chance!

Wrapped up warmly, against the winter chill, I enjoy tidying and pruning in the garden - feeding the fruit bushes now ensures a good crop in the months to come. Dishes served up to guests are all based on seasonal produce, so looking ahead is an essential part of producing the quality that is the hallmark of Cosses. January's favourites are brussel sprouts, swedes, parsnips, leeks, artichokes and winter cabbages still growing in the garden and ready to eat. Stored onions, garlic and shallots are still plentiful.

- Remove from the oven and the bain marie; they will sink back into the cup. Cover with a clean tea towel until needed.
- Preheat oven to 210C.
- Using a knife carefully ease the soufflé from the cup and place upside down on individual gratin dishes. Pour a little single cream over each and sprinkle with parmesan cheese.
- Bake in preheated oven for 5 - 7 mins. until puffed and golden.
- Garnish with rocket and chive or garland chrysanthemum flowers and sprinkle with chopped chives.
- Serve IMMEDIATELY.
- Have your guests sitting at the table before you finish the soufflé as it is better to keep the guests waiting than the soufflé!

- Serve with melba toast or homemade sun dried tomato rolls (see p.89)

Melba Toast

Toast slices of medium sliced bread - brown or white. Whilst still warm, cut off crusts and slice through horizontally; cut each half into two triangles. Place these, untoasted side upwards, under the grill as far from the heat as possible to allow the ends to curl. Toast until pale golden. Store in an airtight container until required.

Gressingham Duckling Breast with Czar Plum Sauce

Braehead Foods a local Ayrshire company supplies our duck, quail, guinea fowl etc.. Gressingham duck is specially bred by one family, to taste like wild duck , but is always tender with not too much fat. The secret of cooking duck is to have crisp fat which tastes delicious and succulent meat. It has often been remarked upon , by our guests that it is the best duck that they have ever tasted!

We grow Victoria and Czar plums at Cosses which freeze very well, straight from the tree (wash, dry and store in freezer bags). This is a simple sauce, complementing the duck perfectly, with just the right amount of sweet and sour.

> 6 Gressingham duckling breasts - medium 200 -225g (7-8oz)
>
> | | |
> |---|---|
> | 1 onion | 1 carrot |
> | 1 parsnip | 1 leek |
> | 1 stick of celery | 600ml (1pt.) |
> | | chicken or pheasant stock |
> | 225g(8oz) Czar plums | 1tbspn. soy sauce |

- Roughly chop the vegetables and place in a casserole dish.
- Score the duck fat in a criss cross fashion (this will help to release the fat) and place the duck skin side up, on the vegetables. Pour around enough stock to reach the base of the duck - the vegetables and stock enhancing the flavour and keeping the duck moist.

(cont'd)

Smoked Haddock Soufflé

Scottish haddock is readily available throughout the winter and naturally smoked has a wonderful flavour. (cold smoked without any added colour). Fresh free range eggs have a deep colour and richer flavour to make this soufflé. It can be prepared ahead of time, then magically puffs out again when reheated to serve.

To serve 6 - 8, butter 6 -8 teacups (inverted pyramid shape)

> 4 large free range eggs - separated
> 300 ml (½pt). béchamel sauce (see page 91)
> 200g (7oz) naturally smoked haddock
> seasoning, pinch of paprika
> 2 tblsp. freshly grated parmesan cheese
> 175ml (6fl.oz.) single cream
> rocket, chives and chive flowers or garland chrysanthemum to garnish

- Preheat oven to 190C.
- Butter an ovenproof dish and place in the haddock, dot with a little more butter and bake in the oven for 5 min. Pour the butter into the teacups to grease them (by swirling the butter around the cup.) Flake the fish removing any of the bones.
- Cook the béchamel sauce stirring all the time, until thick. Remove from the heat and add the flaked fish and seasoning. Beat in 1 egg yolk at a time.
- Meanwhile beat the egg whites until stiff and dry. VERY carefully fold into the fish mixture so as not to lose the bulk of the egg white.
- Boil the kettle for the bain marie. Divide the soufflé mixture between the teacups (they should be ⅚ full), and place in the bain marie.
- Place in the oven and bake at 190C. for 20 -25 mins. until well risen and golden. Your nose will tell you when they are ready! Always a reliable guide in cooking!

- Place in a preheated oven 200C. for 1 hour until the duck is crisp on top.
- Meanwhile simmer the plums in 150ml (5fl.oz.) of stock until soft. Push through a sieve and return the puree to the pan with 1 tblspn soy sauce.
- When the duck is cooked , strain off the liquid into a basin and leave to settle.
- Keep the duck warm.
- Carefully skim the fat off the duck liquid and keep. (It freezes well and is great for roasting potatoes and Yorkshire puddings.)
- Add some of the remaining stock to the plum sauce if necessary. Reheat.
- Slice the duck breasts diagonally into four or five slices and arrange on warm plates with a clapshot garnish, and the rest of the vegetables served separately.
- Pour over a little of the sauce and finish with a little watercress.

(I grow watercress in my potting shed. Some seeds were given to me years ago by my friend Pat Stevenson who brought them from Holland. It keeps growing until really cold weather, and when I remove all the dead vegetation in March, it starts to grow again. It is a great garnish , in salads and soups.)

Clapshot

Traditionally served at this time of year with Haggis to celebrate Burns Night. Our area is famous as the birthplace and home of Robert Burns, born in Alloway on 25th January 1759, he then spent his boyhood 1766-1777 at Mount Oliphant just south of Ayr. In 1775 he went to school in Kirkoswald and some of his best known works are associated with these days i.e.. "Tam o' Shanter" and "Halloween". The "Tam o' Shanter Experience" gives our guests an insight into the life of Robert Burns and the audio visual of the poem "Tam o' Shanter" helps those who are not Scots, to understand the poem. Scottish artist, Alexander Goudie painted the epic poem, now displayed at Rozelle Park .Painted in 1996, he brought Tam o'Shanter to life through wonderful illustrations of the whole poem. Burns Cottage, where he was born, is a museum and there are many other sites relating to the Bard for those who don't want to miss anything.

CLAPSHOT is a mixture of potatoes and swede

750g (1lb. 10 oz) potatoes which mash well e.g. Valor
350g (12oz) swede
4 spring onions or 1 leek
butter and cream
seasoning

- Peel and chop the potatoes and the suede. Place in a pan together with a pinch of salt and boiling water.
- Bring to the boil and simmer for 20 - 30 minutes until cooked. Drain and mash together with butter and cream to taste. Meanwhile finely chop the leek and sauté in a little butter until soft, then add to the potato mixture . Season with pepper. Alternatively, chop the spring onions and add to the potato mixture instead of the leek.

Keep warm then pile into warm vegetable rings (if serving individually) on the warm plate next to the duck. Remove the ring to serve. Or serve in a warm vegetable dish and garnish with the green of the spring onion.

Roast Winter Vegetables

A selection of vegetables roasted in olive oil or duck fat gives them a wonderful flavour. Parsnips, shallots, artichokes and leeks are all plentiful at this time of year; just peel and cut into suitable sizes. Keep the leeks on one side as they do not take very long to cook. Toss in the olive oil or duck fat (about 2 tblspns.) and place in a preheated oven - 200c. for 30 minutes - add leeks , toss again and roast for a further 15 - 20 minutes until all the vegetables are tender. Strain and serve.

Brussel Sprouts

Like all other vegetables , brussel sprouts taste so good straight from the garden - I have even converted those who say that they do not like sprouts! Trim away any marked outer leaves, rinse, then steam for about 5 minutes (depending on the size) until tender. Cut a cross in the base of larger ones.

I steam most of my vegetables on a very high heat for as little time as possible, and I always steam them between courses then serve them straight away, so that all the flavour and the vitamins are retained!

DO NOT keep brassicas warm (or overcook them) as a chemical reaction takes place making them smell! That memory of school dinner cabbage!!

Flambéd Crêpes with pineapple, banana and grapes

For the pancake batter:

115g (4oz) plain flour
25g (1oz) ground almonds
25g (1oz) icing sugar
300ml (10 fl.oz) milk
2 large eggs
2 tblspn kirsch or brandy
1 tblspn sunflower oil

- Place all the ingredients into a blender and liquidize on high for 30 seconds. Scrape down the sides and repeat. Stand for 15 minutes.
- Meanwhile peel a pineapple (widely available from the southern hemisphere at this time of the year), and cut into bite size chunks. Wash and chop the grapes in half- red , black or green, and remove any seeds. Toss in a tblspn of kirsch.
- Not long before serving, peel and slice 2 bananas, and mix with the pineapple and grapes.

(cont'd)

- I have 2 pancake pans which I use for nothing else. I rarely wash them , but just wipe them out with kitchen roll and a little salt. Heat the pans until very hot , swirl around a little sunflower oil- pour out any excess. Heat the oil, then pour in a scoop of pancake batter (a dishwasher scoop is perfect) . Immediately swirl the batter around the pan, so that the mixture just covers the base of the pan. as this sets and bubbles form underneath, lift carefully and flip over with a spatula. The second side will cook in less than a minute. Turn onto a plate. Cook all the pancakes (16-18) and pile them up on top of each other. Cover with a tea towel and they will stay warm for some time.
- Butter a large gratin dish. Take a pancake and place some fruit in the bottom half of it. Fold over one side, then the other to form a point at the bottom; fold the top over to form a triangle. Place fold side down in the dish - continue with as many as you require (2 per person).
- When ready to serve , place in a hot oven 200C. for 5 minutes. Warm 1-2 tblspn kirsch or brandy in a pan, pour over the hot pancakes and flambe by setting alight. Serve with cream or vanilla ice-cream.

Wine at Cosses Country House

Matching food and wine is fun. There is only one certainty: most wine tastes better with most food. Alexander Wines are our suppliers and have put together a selection of wines from all over the wine making world. With each menu of the month, I have included a suggestion from our wine list.

With the duck we selected 'Pinot Noir, Pendarves Estate, Hunter Valley, Australia'.

'A practising GP and vocal advocate of wine drinking as a way to better health, Dr. Phil Norrie, shows what can be achieved with the fickle Pinot noir in Australia's Lower Hunter Valley. The limestone soil of his vineyards - unusual in the Hunter, where most soils are volcanic - seems to be just what this temperamental grape needs to perform. A juicy mouthful of ripe, spiced berry fruits and firm but rounded tannins that more than does justice to game and rich red meats...'

FEBRUARY

Sunset over Ailsa Craig & Kintyre Peninsula
(Watercolour)
Susan Crosthwaite

Menu:

Cream of Artichoke Soup or Minestrone Soup
Home-made bread rolls
Lemon Sole with Tomato and Parsley sauce garnished
with Tomatoes filled with Petit Pois
Duchesse potatoes, Early Purple Sprouting Broccoli
Warm Pear and Almond Tarte Crème Anglaise with
Home-made Ice Cream
Scottish Cheese with Homemade Oatcakes

FEBRUARY

W e often get beautiful crisp days in February followed by wonderful sunsets as seen in the painting. The drive down the Ayrshire coast from Turnberry to Ballantrae is quite spectacular (especially into the sunset) and has been compared to the Californian coastline by some of our American guests.

'Carrick', the name of our area, signifies the area of the rock, ie.- the area from whose coastline Ailsa Craig is always visible. Galloway originally incorporated the whole of Southwest Scotland, from the Clyde to the Solway - it was first split in 1186 by the Scottish King William the Lion when Carrick was given to Duncan McDowall de Carrick, (probably in return for services rendered in Northumbria by his father Gilbert during an invasion) whilst his cousin Roland Lord of Galloway (the rightful heir) was only allowed Galloway - (as we know today!). Duncan and Roland were grandsons of Fergus Mac Dubh Ghael, the greatest Lord of Galloway, born in 1096 and died in 1161. Fergus married Elizabeth, daughter of Henry 1 of England (granddaughter of William the Conqueror), and they had 4 children. Three of these children founded genealogical branches which had astonishing records in the history of Great Britain and will be explored throughout the following chapters. Duncan was the son of Gilbert - Fergus and Elizabeth's second son. He had a long reign as Lord of Carrick and founded Crossaguel Abbey in 1193 (just south of Maybole). In 1225, he was created the 1st Earl of Carrick and he acquired wide lands in Ireland which he named after his grandfather - Carrick Fergus. Duncan was succeeded by Neil who died in 1256 and whose daughter and heiress Marjory, married Robert de Bruce, the 7th Lord of Annandale. Their eldest son Robert the Bruce became King of Scots 1306 - 1329. He was probably born at Turnberry Castle, though Lochmaben (near Dumfries) and Writtle (near Chelmsford in Essex), both lay claim to his birthplace.

Turnberry is perhaps the most probable as it was in this vicinity that the romance between his father and mother occurred; and it was here that his heart lay , and where the early struggles for Scottish freedom were centred. While he owned lands near London, Essex, Yorkshire, Annandale and at Turnberry, his Scottish patriotism was ignited by the traditions of his mother's heritage. On 20th September 1286 the first recorded meeting of Scottish Nobles took place at Turnberry Castle in support of Bruce to become King of Scotland. The English occupied Turnberry Castle in 1307, but were routed after the battle of Glen Trool. The castle was badly damaged by the English, but was later restored by Bruce. Just north of Ballantrae, near Balig, stands a stone windmill which was where all the village grain was milled, (this windmill was one of the few buildings of stone, other than the castles, all the others were made of wood). When the English tried to invade via Ireland , Robert the Bruce had all the homes and crops burnt so that there would be nothing for the English to eat or plunder. Although Bruce deserted William Wallace, and changed allegiances several times; after Wallace's death, Bruce led the Scottish army to victory at Bannockburn, and became their King.

Robert's younger brother, Edward de Bruce , held the titles Lord of Galloway, Earl of Carrick and King of Ireland , but he was slain at Dundalk in 1318. Robert the Bruce by his first marriage to Isabella, had a daughter named Marjory (after her grandmother). She married Walter Steuart, who founded Paisley Abbey, and their son - Robert Steuart became Robert 11 , King of Scots and first of the Royal Stewarts. The title of Earl of Carrick was given to his son John Stewart in 1368 and merged with the crown when he became King Robert 111 in 1390. The title Earl of Carrick is presently held by H.R.H. Prince Charles, and as explained in chapter 12 the present Royal family are descendants of this family, and thus the Lords of Galloway.

Despite the association of the Earls of Carrick with the Crown, the principal power in Carrick became vested in the Kennedies, who were also descendants of Fergus Mac dubh Ghael, through Roland who was the above mentioned Duncan's cousin - see chapter 7.

The best place to view the whole of Carrick and Galloway and its coastline is within walking distance from Cosses. Beneraird, 1435 feet and the highest point in the immediate area, means 'chief pinnacle of the mountain area'. Once a considerable Cairn (stone fortification) stood on it's peak. The old road from Ballantrae to New Luce runs by its summit, but one must not stray as a huge morass of bog haggs surrounds the summit. There are spectacular 360 degree views, from the Isle of Man to Arran and a vast panorama of mountains, valleys and moorlands from the Carricks to the Merricks and Mountains of Fleet. It is a great shame that this road has not been made passable to tourists in cars to enable them to enjoy some of the most spectacular views in Scotland only available to those who walk or cycle.

Girvan (formally Known as Invergarvane) is the largest town in Carrick today having overtaken Maybole in the 19th century. A place of some antiquity, it has one of the few safe harbours on the Carrick coast thus fishing along with cotton weaving developed. A small boat builders yard, Alexander Noble and Sons, was established in 1946. While most of the boats have gone to work in local waters, others have been built for owners as far afield as Cornwall and the outer Hebrides and more recently, the yard has diversified building boats for fish farms as well as repair work. In 1964 William Grant and Sons began production of grain whisky from a new distillery at Grangestone in Girvan. It is from here that the local spirit is now married to the twenty or so Highland malts which give Grant's Standfast its unique character. The famous blend in the distinctive triangular bottle, is dispatched around the world from Girvan and 'neutral spirit' is produced as gin and vodka.

Back at Cosses, during February, clearing and tidying the garden and woodland keep us busy. Snowdrops are now joined by crocus and daffodils, the vibernum pink blooms look like spring blossom and the early daphne's give wonderful scent. The plaintive cries of the buzzard can be heard during the short winter days and the Tawny and Barn owls at night. Roe deer visit to supplement their diet so new trees need to be protected.

Good soup making is a must for the winter, making use of all the winter vegetables. Artichokes (Jerusalem) make a great winter standby, (the tubers should be left in the ground until February—lift as required until then—then lift and replant as many as required) and minestrone remains a firm family favourite.

Cream of Artichoke Soup

500g Jerusalem Artichokes - peeled
2 onions, chopped   25g butter
700 ml chicken stock (see page 91)
300 ml milk   seasoning
cream (optional)   fresh chives

- Melt the butter and sweat the onions then add the chopped artichokes and mix with the onions. Add the stock, bring to the boil and simmer for 40 minutes.
- Add the milk and bring back to the boil. Liquidise then check seasoning.
- Reheat when ready to serve. This soup freezes well.
- Serve with a swirl of single cream and snipped chives, with home-made bread rolls.

Minestrone Soup

1 onion	2 tblspn olive oil
2 cloves garlic	1 leek
1 carrot	1 small swede
1 parsnip	2 sticks celery
½ red pepper	¼ green cabbage
small tin baked beans	1 tin tomatoes, pureed

1 wine glass of red wine
1 tsp. dried basil and fresh basil to serve
1.2 litre chicken or pheasant stock (see page 91)
Parmesan cheese served separately

- Finely chop all the vegetables except the cabbage then sweat in the olive oil until beginning to soften. Add the stock, wine and pureed tomatoes. Bring to the boil.
- Add dried basil, salt and pepper and simmer for 30-40 minutes. Add the shredded cabbage and the baked beans for the last 5 minutes.
- Best left for the flavours to infuse - when cold, refrigerate.
- Reheat to serve sprinkled with fresh basil, parmesan served separately, and garlic bread.

Lemon Sole with tomato and parsley sauce garnished with tomatoes filled with petit pois. Duchesse potatoes, early purple sprouting broccoli

Any fish that I cannot get through the local fishermen is supplied by Pieroni & Sons of Ayr, a wholesale and retail fish supplier who deliver to Ballantrae on Tuesdays and Fridays.

Approx. 175g (6oz) sole per person (700g for 4)
lemon juice
75 ml (2½ fl.oz) white wine
pepper
butter
freshly chopped parsley
300ml (½ pint) béchamel sauce (see page 91)
1 tblspn double cream
4 tomatoes each skinned and seeded

- Remove any bones from the fish and cut larger fillets in half lengthways (2 - 3 per person).
- Squeeze lemon juice onto back of fish and season with pepper.
- Roll up (skin side to the inside). Butter an ovenproof dish and place fish into it. Sprinkle over the wine and dot with butter and bake for 10 minutes at 200C.
- Meanwhile, skin the tomatoes by pouring over boiling water, count for 30 seconds and then plunge into cold water. The skins should peel off easily. Cut into quarters and discard the seeds into a bowl through a sieve to reserve any juice. Add this to the béchamel sauce.
- Cut quarters of tomatoes in half, lengthways.
- Make the béchamel sauce by bringing to the boil stirring constantly.
- Add some of the fish liqueur from the cooked sole to make the sauce a pouring consistency.
- Add tomatoes and parsley.
- Serve around the sole garnished with ½ tomatoes stuffed with petit pois.

For the stuffed tomatoes

- Cut large tomatoes in half and with a grapefruit knife carefully remove the pulp (reserve for stock or soup). Dot with butter or oil and place on a baking sheet and bake with the fish for 5 minutes.
- Meanwhile steam the petit pois for 5 minutes and serve in tomato shells topped with a mint leaf.

Duchesse potatoes

7-800 g (1¾lb) potatoes peeled	25g (1oz) butter
1 tblspn cream	1 egg yolk
salt, pepper,	
nutmeg (freshly grated)	

- Cook potatoes for 20-30 minutes in boiling salted water then strain. Mash or sieve adding the remaining ingredients. Pipe whilst still hot onto a buttered baking sheet. Refrigerate until ready to use.
- Bake for 10 minutes at 200C then serve garnished with parsley.
- Early purple sprouting broccoli is one of the most delicious of broccoli. It starts sprouting in February and various varieties keep going until June when the first summer broccoli is ready. It is possible to have different types of broccoli in the garden all year round.
- Just steam the vegetables between courses (a bit like soufflés) - it is better to keep the guests waiting a few minutes than have overcooked vegetables (just as bad undercooked!).

(cont'd)

Warm Pear and Almond Tarte Crème Anglaise

6 ripe pears (we grow Conference and Williams)
Juice of 1 lemon

For pastry:

225g (8oz) plain flour 140g (5oz) butter, chopped
pinch of salt   1 tblspn sugar
2 tblspn cold water   1 egg, separated

- Rub butter into sifted flour with sugar and salt until fine bread crumbs (I use my k beater on my Kenwood). Add the egg yolk mixed with the water to form a ball of dough. Wrap in cling film and chill for 30 minutes.
- Roll out and line 4 individual flan tins or one 7 inch. Brush with beaten egg white, chill again.

For the Almond Cream

25g (1oz) icing sugar   55g (2oz) ground almonds
25g (1oz) butter   ½ beaten egg
3 tblspn single cream

- Combine the icing sugar, softened butter and ground almonds (in the Kenwood), add enough egg to make a soft cream. Spread half this mixture on the pastry base. Reserve the rest.
- Peel and core the pears and slice lengthways, dip in lemon juice and arrange decoratively on the almond cream base. Brush with more lemon juice.
- Bake the tart 200C for 20 minutes. Mix the single cream with the rest of the almond cream.
- Spread over the cooked tart and then place under a hot grill until golden.
- Serve with homemade ice cream.
- Garnish with pear leaf by cutting three long v-shaped notches in a quarter of a pear, skin side up, each notch slightly larger than the one before. Push each piece along on top of the one below to form a leaf shape. Brush with lemon juice.

Rueda Blanco Especial, Con Class, DO, Spain is the suggested wine to complement this menu.

'From Rueda in north-central Spain, this bright young white from the dynamic Ricardo Sanz combines the crispness of Viura with the nuttiness of Verdejo. Fresh and zingy, with a vivid gooseberry tang, this is a punchy, immediate style combining local traditions with a decidedly 'New World' twist.'

March

Daffodils & Cosses Bridge
(Watercolour)
Susan Crosthwaite

Menu:

Striped Mousseline of Salmon and Sole
with Sauce Newburg
Roast locally reared Sirloin of Beef
Yorkshire Pudding, fresh Horseradish Sauce
Roast Potatoes and Shallots
Carrots and Leeks
Spring Cabbage and Ginger
Meringue Nests filled with Fresh Fruit and served
with Melba Sauce
Scottish Cheese and Homemade Oatcakes

MARCH

Daffodils abound prolifically during March forming a thick golden carpet around the garden and along the banks of Crailoch Burn. Endless bunches are picked to welcome spring into the house along with the new season's visitors.

Threave Gardens at Castle Douglas are famous for their spectacular selection of daffodils in bloom with winter heathers and other spring bulbs and are open all year round.

On a cold blustery March day a visit to the Gem Rock Museum at Creetown, is a must. It houses one of the finest private collections of gem stones, crystals, minerals, and fossils in Britain. Owned and run by the Stephenson family , the museum is designed to stimulate interest and wonder in the fascinating subjects of gems ,crystals and mineralogy. There is a truly astonishing display of natural mineral forms in every conceivable shape colour and size, together with a volcanic eruption display and a 15 minute audio programme to introduce visitors to the museum. There are huge specimens of quartz and fluorite crystal groups, exquisite geodes lined with amethysts, agates with dazzling colour bands, opals and even diamonds. There is a fossilised dinosaur egg and a meteorite from outer space. The 'working minerals' used by mankind for centuries, include the copper group - malachite, azurite and cuprite; the red ores of kidney - like haematite magnetites, asbestos, ironstone, tin and lead as well as many more exotic minerals. The gift shop specialises in gemstones and jewellery , many worked on within the museum's workshop where the art of Lapidary can be viewed.

The coastal area around Ballantrae extends from the peat covered moorlands of the Scottish Southern Uplands to the attractive rocky coastline of South Ayrshire. Within it an unusual assemblage of igneous rocks reveals the existence of a long vanished Ordovician ocean. The adjacent late Ordovician sedimentary rocks range from deep water turbidites in the south to neritic conglomerate and limestone in the north. Their transgressive overlap of the igneous rocks illustrates the submurgence of the ocean margin. The Ballantrae area provides a fascinating insight into dramatic geological processes and is a source of study for many geology students.

Fossils have been discovered at Hawkhead quarry, near Dailly, which match fossils found in the Appalachian Mountains in North America. This gives credence to the theory by geologists that, 60 million years ago, Scotland was ripped off the north American continent following a series of massive volcanic eruptions; the last remaining evidence of this being the volcanic plug of Ailsa Craig. More recently, footprints of a dinosaur have been found at Staffin, on the Isle of Skye, matching footprints of an identical dinosaur in Wyoming, America again adding weight to the theory that Scotland was once linked to America.

Many interesting gem rocks at the museum have been found on the shore between Ballantrae and Girvan. Special places of interest include Kennedy Pass, Slockenray, Pinbain Bridge, Bonney's Dyke, Carlton Fishery, Games Loup, Balcreuchan Port and Bennane Head .

In the meantime, demands of the garden continue, preparing ground and planting potatoes, onion sets etc. Leeks are still in the ground and spring cabbages are just beginning but it is not a notable time of the year for any special home-grown produce. We are lucky to have an abundant supply of fresh fish and beef the whole year round.

Striped Mousseline of Salmon and Sole with Sauce Newburg

225g (8oz) Salmon fillet, chopped
225g (8oz) Sole fillet, chopped
Optional - lobster, crab or prawns

3 eggs	450 ml (16fl.oz) double cream
Seasoning	300 ml (10fl.oz) fish stock
	(see page 91) reduced to
	2 tblspn
Butter	1 tsp., level, paprika
150 ml (5fl.oz) double cream	

- All the ingredients must be ice cold for this dish.
- Blend the salmon in a liquidiser or blender adding half the eggs. Repeat with the sole and chill for at least an hour. Butter non-stick pudding moulds or line 8 ramekins with cling film.
- With a balloon whisk gradually add ½ chilled cream to salmon puree. Season. Repeat for sole.
- Spoon some salmon mixture into each ramekin or mould (a layer of prawns, lobster meat or crab meat can be added at this point - optional). Spoon over sole mixture.
- Cover with overlapping cling or foil and keep in the fridge until ready to cook.
- Steam for 10 minutes in fierce steam.
- Meanwhile melt the butter and gently cook paprika. Add the reduced fish stock and cream and heat gently. Turn out the fish creams onto warm plates and surround with the sauce. Garnish with fresh dill.

Roast locally reared Sirloin of Beef, Yorkshire Pudding, Fresh Horseradish Sauce, Roast Potatoes and Shallots, Carrots and Leeks, Spring Cabbage and Ginger

Good beef is still a firm favourite with our guests. I have been using the same local butcher, Mr McFadzean of Dalduff Farm, Crosshill, since we first came to Cosses in 1985. He raises his own beef and lamb, bred and raised here in the Ayrshire hills and sold through his farm shop. The beef is from native breeds such as Aberdeen Angus, Bluegrays and Galloway crosses.

Mr McFadzean says that good husbandry, healthy breeding, careful handling then a well hung carcass produces the best beef. Sirloin on or off the bone is my favourite for roasting as it has a certain amount of fat which is essential for tenderness and flavour. Allow 225g (8oz) on the bone and 175g (6oz) off, per person.

- The meat should be at room temperature before cooking. Preheat the oven to 220C. Preheat roasting tin. Sprinkle the beef with finely ground black pepper. Place in hot roasting tin in the oven and roast for the first 10 minutes at 220C then reduce to 200C.
- For rare, allow 15 minutes per pound or 450g and 15 minutes over.
- Medium to well done, 20 minutes per pound or 450 g and 20 minutes over.

- Cooking times may vary according to the thickness of the joint. Plan the cooking time to allow the meat to "rest" for 15 minutes keeping it warm whilst the vegetables are finished and the gravy made with the juices from the roasting tin.
- Pour the cooking liquid from the vegetables into the roasting tin (having removed the beef), scrape the sediment from the tin and pour into a pan. Thicken with cornflour mixed with a little cold water.

Yorkshire Puddings

With my Yorkshire origins I couldn't miss out on this recipe! It is so very easy - the secret being a really hot oven and well proved tins.

To prove the tins, place in the oven whilst the beef is cooking for a while. If I don't have beef dripping duck fat makes an excellent substitute (also for the potatoes).

2 eggs - large
115g (4oz) plain flour
300 ml(½ pt) milk
½ tsp. salt

- Liquidise ingredients for 30 seconds and stand for at least 15 minutes. After removing the beef from the oven put a little beef or duck fat (or oil) in each pudding tin and place in the oven (preheated to 220C) until smoking.
- Pour in the batter mixture and bake for approximately 10 minutes (longer for larger puddings) until well risen and brown. Serve immediately.

Horseradish Cream

Horseradish grows like a weed (a dock leaf) when established. Every gardener should have a clump, if only to experience how indifferent the bottled variety is. It is rich in vitamin C and minerals and is a natural antibiotic, appetite stimulant and digestive. Just dig up a bit of root as required, peel and grate.

- Add freshly grated horseradish to single cream with lemon juice to taste.

Roast potatoes and shallots

- Peel the potatoes and cut into suitable sizes, keep in water. Peel shallots (in water if they make you cry). Preheat the roasting tin with dripping, duck fat or oil (2 tblspn). Dry the potatoes well. Toss in fat in the roasting tin and roast for 1 hour turning from time to time. Add the shallots after 30 minutes. Serve around the beef.

Steamed carrots and leeks

- Peel and cut the carrots into thin strips. Wash the leeks well and cut diagonally. Steam together for 5 minutes until carrots are just tender. Sprinkle with parsley to serve. The leeks enhance the flavour of the carrots.

(cont'd)

Steamed spring cabbage with ginger

- Wash the cabbage and remove the coarse stalk. Shred by tearing or slice with a serrated knife. Finely chop 1 inch of ginger root, peeled, and mix in the cabbage.
- Steam for 2 to 3 minutes until just tender. Toss with black pepper and serve immediately.

Meringue Nests filled with fresh fruit served with melba sauce

A firm favourite with many of our guests and looks almost too good to eat. Use the fruit in season and many exotic fruits which are available from the southern continents and warmer climates.

Meringues are easy to make if a few rules are followed. They keep well in an airtight container or freezer.

Eggs must be at room temperature - egg whites freeze well. Implements must be grease free. Once the whisking begins don't stop until the meringue is in the oven. Cook in preheated oven to set meringue.

Always use 55g (2oz) sugar to each egg white. Granulated sugar is so fine these days it is not necessary to use caster sugar.

3 egg whites	½ tsp. cornflour
175g (6oz) sugar	¼ tsp. vanilla extract
¼ tsp. of white vinegar	

- Beat the egg whites on full in a Kenwood for about 5 minutes. Very slowly (sprinkle a teaspoon at a time) add the sugar whilst the Kenwood is still on full. Finally add the cornflour, vinegar and vanilla. Place in a large piping bag fitted with a star nozzle and pipe baskets by starting in the middle and doing a spiral for 3 round outwards then 3 high.
- Bake at 150C for 10 minutes then reduce the heat to 110C. for 45 minutes. Leave in the oven to cool to prevent cracking.
- Store until needed.

Melba Sauce (see page 92)

- Fill each meringue with some crème fraiche (a tangy contrast to the sweetness of meringue) and arrange the fruit e.g. section of pineapple, slice kiwifruit, slice papaya, ½ apricot or plum, ¼ pear, slices of peach, banana cut diagonally, whole strawberries, cherries and grapes.
- Use some fruit alongside the melba sauce for garnish. Serve.

Ch. Villars, Costieres de Nimes, France is the choice to complement the roast Sirloin of Beef.
'Coming from the West of Chateauneuf-du-Pape and in a similar style, this wine is made up of 30% Grenache, 55% Syrah and 12% Mouvedre, all of which contribute something towards the delicate violet and honey nose and flavour of ripe soft fruits. Owned by the Bois family, whose estate, which overlooks the Camargue, is the envy of its neighbours.'

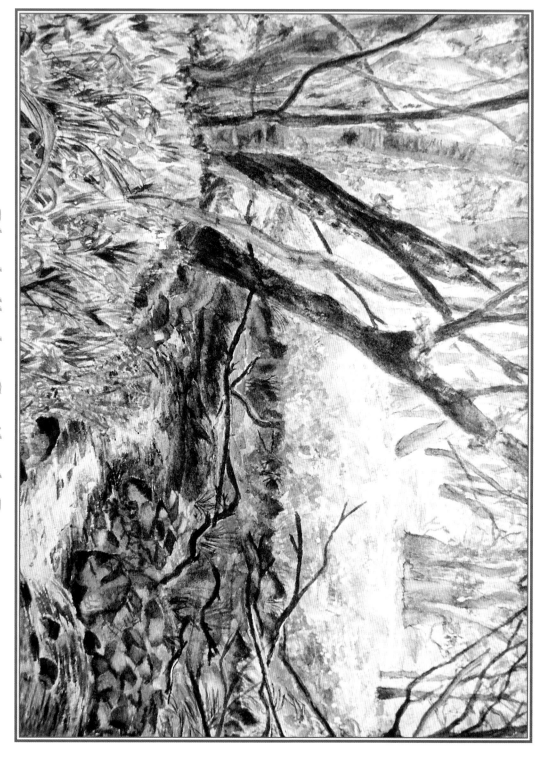

APRIL

Bluebells by Crailoch Burn

(*Watercolour*)
Susan Crosthwaite

Menu:

Monkfish, Prawns and Scallops in a
Light Saffron sauce with Seakale
Fillet of Loin of Ayrshire Lamb roast with Garlic,
Ginger and Rosemary, and finished with
Madeira and Redcurrant Sauce.
Garden herb stuffed mushrooms
Cauliflower florettes, Swiss Chard, Rosemary
and Garlic new potatoes.
Summer Pudding

APRIL

Spring is here! The birds are building nests , everyone is busy planting seeds, fields are being ploughed and sown, new born lambs frolic together while the last bits of spring cleaning have to be completed as we become busier with our guests. The woodland awakens with anemones, wild orchids and bluebell. Follow the deer track through the woods and discover spring in every nook and cranny.

Cosses provides a huge selection of nesting places for the many birds to be found in this area, with over 120 varieties being listed. At the mouth of the River Stinchar and along the shoreline a 55 acre reserve was established in 1969 by the Scottish Wildlife Trust to protect the small nesting colony of the little tern. Grassland, mud flats and shingle provide resident and migratory birds with a variety of feeding and nesting sites. Oyster catcher and ringed plover nests are well concealed amongst fine sand and pebbles. Nearby mud flats and tidelines are a rich source of food. The long red bill of the oyster catcher is an ideal tool for probing amongst the soft mud. Red shank , dunlin and curlew often join the search for invertebrates. Red breasted mergansers haunt the marsh channels and hollows hidden along the rank grassy banks to use as nests where a dozen buff coloured eggs may be laid. Overhead sand martins weave intricate patterns in their pursuit of flies. Ever opportunistic they have exploited the eroding southern bank of the river to establish a colony. The adept mimicry of our most common wetland warbler, the sedge warbler, and the insect like song of the grasshopper warbler may surprise the off guard listener.

Four of the five breeding Scottish species of tern; arctic, common, little and sandwich, can be seen within the reserve, or fishing offshore. Although all have formerly bred, only two, the arctic tern and the little tern still breed. As the arctic tern is Scotland's second rarest seabird this small colony at Ballantrae is of national significance.

Heron thrive prolifically and nest at the end of Laggan woods; it is a sight to behold, this huge bird rising from the water with a fish in its beak. The small clachan of Heronsford is sited at the end of Laggan woods and the bridge over the Water of Tigg. Overhead the skylark sings as it soars . Offshore, the imposing form of Ailsa Craig dominates as diving gannets fish in spectacular fashion. Ailsa Craig and Scare Rocks (off the Mull of Galloway), and the cliffs on the Mull itself provide nesting sites for puffins, guillemots, razorbills and fulmar.

Robin's father was an ornithologist and he leased the Scare rocks where 2,000 pairs of gannets breed, and Robin remembers him filming puffins. The rocks reverted to the R.S.P.B. when Robin's father J.H. Stainton Crosthwaite died in 1972. He was a joint editor, along with John Fraser and C. Eric Palmar, of 'Birds of Britain', and they were founder members of the British Ornithologists Union. One of the stories from booklet No.2 by Stainton is about filming the fulmar on the cliffs of the Mull of Galloway: '......we walked onwards and soon reached the fulmar's cove. The Irish coast and the far away mountains of Mourne had a lovely mistiness about them. A long way below, skimming the sea, cormorants, shags, razorbills and guillimots flew. Round a headland a peregrine dashed. Suddenly, sailing along, with wings held straight out, came the bird we were after — the Fulmar. It was gliding buoyantly above the cliffs, complete master of the fierce air currents. It's wings had not the 'elbow - bend' of a gull; it's blue-grey back, together with it's white head and neck, matched the white-horsed waves below. The Fulmar colony , of which this bird was only the advance guard, I filmed from their leisurely courtship days to their serious family cares. Most attention was given to a nest which was some thirty feet down this two hundred feet cliff . During courtship, two birds held each other's beaks, swaying gently backwards and forwards. They would also bow repeatedly, uttering at the same time soft grunts, followed by a loud cackling serenade in which both held their heads upwards, with beaks wide open ....The one white egg, about three inches long , reclined upon the plain earth, with little stones at the seaward edge; it showed faint rust coloured patches ....and there crouching flat, was a chick, plump and covered with whitish-grey down. At this early stage it darted it's head at my stroking hand. But a month later it squirted out a stream of amber - coloured oil when approached! ....I ringed this now very fat, all grey youngster. ....'

At Cosses we enjoy discovering the huge variety of nesting places, the blue tits in the half tyres protecting the horses from the corner of the fence; swallows and house martins in the eves, the barns and the stables; the beech hedge is the home to many different birds, and warblers nest on top of a post in the wood shed. Ducks nest safely on the island in the pond, and it is a great treat to watch the mother duck teaching the ducklings to swim up the burn and negotiate the many hurdles.

Spring cabbages, cauliflower and purple sprouting broccoli, dormant over the winter, suddenly bloom and provide us with delicious fresh vegetables. Swiss Chard takes on a new lease of life and sends up a second crop of fresh leaves. Seakale, forced under buckets (tastes a little like asparagus) is a rare delicacy for our taste buds.

Tulips, spring heather, pulmonaria and muscari join the daffodils, while primroses grow wild in abundance on all the hillsides, especially those facing the sea on the drive between Ballantrae and Girvan. We still have cowslips- a great edible garnish.

Cosses being situated in the middle of farmland shares the joys and dramas of the lambing season. Bobby our neighbouring farmer brings his sheep into the lambing sheds as their lambs are due. The whole process is supervised, so that triplets can be twinned on to ewes with a single lamb and any ewe having a problem can be helped along. As soon as the little family is fit they are transported, in the specially designed trailer, behind the 4 wheeler motorbike to the nearby fields of fresh juicy new grass.

Monkfish, Prawns and Scallops in a light saffron sauce with Seakale

55g(2oz) butter
24 medium prawns or langoustines
8 small escalopes, or 4 large sliced in half - horizontally.
16 scallops of monkfish (1 medium tail)
125ml (4fl.oz) fish stock (see page 91)
½ wine glass of white wine
good pinch of saffron
150ml (5fl.oz) double cream
115g (4oz) seakale
Dill to garnish
(see page 76 for prawn preparation)

- It is just the tail of the monkfish which is eaten - the head and body are large and flat and are discarded. Monkfish tails are easily prepared - just slide a sharp knife down either side of the bone and using the knife ease off the skin. Slice into escalopes.
- To clean the scallops - using a small sharp knife twist it at either side of the base of the shell to break the muscle and slide around the inside of the shell to release. Using the knife , carefully ease off the scallop meat and the coral (if liked) and rinse away any grit, veins and skin. Slice large scallops in half.
- Prepare the fish and chill until half an hour before cooking (all fish should be at room temperature to cook).
- Soak the saffron in the fish stock for 1 hour, then reduce to about 1 tablespoon over a high heat.
- Heat the frying pan and when hot drop in a third of the butter and sear the scallops on either side until coloured, keep warm. Melt the remaining butter in the frying pan and sauté the prepared monk fish and prawns, for 4-5 minutes until just cooked. Remove to a warm dish and keep warm.

- Add the white wine and the reduced saffron infused stock to the frying pan and reduce further to 2tblspn. Finally add the cream and heat until bubbling.
- Meanwhile steam the seakale for 4-5 minutes.
- On warm plates, arrange the prawns, scallops and monkfish with the seakale as a garnish, drizzle the sauce over the fish finishing with a little dill. Serve immediately.

Fillet of Loin of Ayrshire Lamb roasted with garlic, ginger and rosemary, and finished with Madeira and Redcurrant sauce.

The lamb, like the beef is bred and raised on the Ayrshire hills, from Suffolk, Texel and Blackface crosses. Healthy breeding, handling and the best of husbandry with complete traceability of all stock are the foundations of good Scottish lamb.

1 boned loin of lamb (a boned loin usually weighs between 550-700g)
1 garlic clove
1 small piece of fresh ginger
2 sprigs of Rosemary

- The butcher will bone out the loin of lamb. Pull the skin from the meat and trim the membrane as you would do with a fillet of beef.
- Finely chop the ginger and the garlic and rub into the lamb. Place in a roasting tin on top of the rosemary (retaining some for garnish). Cover and chill until 1 hour before cooking. To seal with cling film, rub a little oil around the edge of the tin, then press down the cling, so that the smell of garlic and ginger does not invade the fridge!

For the sauce:

150ml (5fl.oz) demi glace sauce (see page 91)
55g (2oz) redcurrants
1 wine glass Madeira wine
1 tspn redcurrant jelly
to serve redcurrant jelly (see page 92)

To cook the lamb:
- Remove cling film.
- Preheat the oven to 200C. Place the lamb in the oven for 20 minutes.
- Pour over the Madeira and roast for a further 5 minutes. Meanwhile heat the demi glace sauce with the teaspoon of redcurrant jelly. Remove the lamb from the oven and pour the juices into the sauce. Reduce slightly and then add the redcurrants, having reserved a few for garnish. (Redcurrants should be picked and frozen in sprigs. Whilst still frozen, strip from the stalk and rinse - reserve some on the stalks for garnish)
- Slice the fillet into 4 or 5 slices per person, arrange on warm plates and pour over some of the sauce. Garnish with sprigs of rosemary and redcurrants. Serve the rest of the sauce separately along with a bowl of redcurrant jelly.

Garden herb stuffed mushrooms

1 large or 2 medium mushrooms per person
1 spring onion per person
1 tspn bread crumbs per person
mixed fresh herbs finely chopped
25g (1oz) butter
seasoning

- Melt the butter in a frying pan, and dip the mushrooms into it, having carefully removed the stalks. Coat with melted butter and place on a baking dish.
- Chop the stalks (if the stalks are very small , use an extra mushroom) and the spring onions and add to the frying pan, sauté lightly, then add the remaining ingredients. Mix well , then pile into the mushroom caps.
- To serve: place in a preheated oven (200C.) for 5 minutes. Use as a garnish.

Cauliflower, fresh from the garden and broken into florets, only takes a minute to steam on a high heat. Add a little purple sprouting broccoli for a contrast in colour (be careful that the purple does not run into the cauliflower). Cook between courses and serve immediately.

Swiss Chard is one of those very useful vegetables that is worth its weight in gold as it grows in the garden the whole year round in our mild climate. It is also available in a variety of colours. Sown in April, it is ready in June and provides spinach like leaves with edible stems over the summer with a second flush in the spring , before going to seed. Wash it well, then chop the stems and tear the leaves or slice with a serrated knife.
- Steam for 5 minutes. Season with salt, pepper and nutmeg.

Rosemary and garlic potatoes

New early Egyptian and Jersey potatoes are usually available at this time.

900g (2lb) potatoes
40g (1½oz)duck fat or olive oil
2 garlic cloves
3-4 sprigs rosemary
seasoning

- Wash the potatoes and dry well. Heat the duck fat in a roasting tin.
- Split the garlic cloves into 4. Place the potatoes, garlic and rosemary in the roasting tin and toss well. Roast for 45-60 minutes. Season to taste and serve garnished with fresh rosemary.

Summer Pudding

Using all the fruits from the freezer this has a wonderful taste of the summer. Defrost the fruit before cooking.

Homebaked or fresh uncut white bread (see page 88)

115g (4oz) strawberries
115g (4oz) raspberries
115g (4oz) blackcurrants
115 g(4oz) redcurrants
115g (4oz) blackberries
115g (4oz) stoned plums -quartered
115g (4oz)sugar

- Place the fruit, except the strawberries and the raspberries, in a pan with the sugar and heat gently until the juices run and the fruit is just cooked. Add the strawberries and raspberries to the hot fruit and stir.
- Meanwhile slice the bread, remove the crusts and flatten with a rolling pin. Line ramekins, teacups or chinese bowls with cling film overlapping the edges.
- Press the rolled bread to fit the lined bowls — cut off the excess and fit into any spaces.
- Using a pastry cutter, cut a lid of rolled bread for each bowl.
- Fill each bread lined bowl with warm mixed fruit using plenty of juice to soak into the bread.
- Place a bread lid on each bowl. Add a little more juice and seal with overlapping cling film. Place a heavy weight on each pudding i.e.. a tin of beans or a 2lb weight! Leave for at least 2 hours, then chill overnight or for several hours. Turnout of the bowl and discard the cling. Serve garnished with extra fruit compote and a sprig of mint. Serve with single cream, sauce anglais, (see page 66) or ice cream (see page 94).

Wine of the month:

Gran Campellas Tinto Crianza, Bodegas Borsao, Campo de Borja, Spain

'The name 'Campo de Borja' may not trip off the tongue with quite the same ease as Rioja, but this is just one of Spanish regions currently producing top quality reds to challenge Rioja's long-standing dominance in that area. A masterly blend of Garnacha, Tempranillo and Cabernet, this mature, velvety Reserva has the softness that comes from extended ageing in barrel combined with a dark, savoury fruitiness that goes perfectly with lamb and red meats generally.'

MAY

Dogs in the Bluebell Woods

(*Watercolour*)
Susan Crosthwaite

ℳenu:

Caesar Salad
Fresh Halibut with Sorrel sauce
Mousseline of Spinach
Pommes de terre Forestière
Brandy Snap Cones filled with
Rhubarb Fool served with
Rhubarb and Ginger sauce

May

May, with it's record for fine weather and long days is by far my favourite month. Nature is at its busiest and best, bird song fills the air as the swallows and house martins return to their nesting places, the sound of the cuckoo as it lays its eggs for an unawary mother bird to hatch and feed, and the song thrushes add their notes in the evening air.

Some of our guests enjoy taking part in the daily ritual of walking Bonzo (our black labrador), a friendly chap, who loves to race through the woods carpeted with anemones, bluebells and wild orchids, a particular joy at this time. There is always a new natural drama unfolding, whether it be a chance meeting with a deer, a darting rabbit or hare, or the sudden vocal flight of a startled pheasant. It all happens —— providing endless delight.

Many visitors come specifically to enjoy Cosses springtime and wander, at leisure, the numerous gardens, displaying azaleas and rhododendrons. One of these is Glenwhan at Dunragit, with it's commanding views over Luce Bay and the Mull of Galloway. This young garden was started in 1979 by Tessa Knott, hewn from a hillside covered in bracken, gorse (whin) and rushes (Glenwhan means 'glen or the rushes'). With exceptional vision, energy and skill she transformed it into 12 acres of spectacular garden featuring rhododendrons, azaleas , shrubs and many unusual plants which grow happily together around 2 small lochans, (made by damming up the boggy areas) plus a whole cascading chain of pools and waterfalls.. A water garden creates a natural habitat for the bog loving generea and the rocky outcrops are home for alpines and scree plants, heathers etc. Combine a visit here with Castle Kennedy Gardens and Logan Botanical gardens (all very different) and you have a spectacular day out for any garden lover.

Broughton House and garden is another favourite of mine, being the home and studio of E A Hornel (a leading artist of a group known as the Glasgow Boys). The house contains many of his works, along with paintings of other contemporary artists, and an extensive collection of rare Scottish books, including limited editions of Burns works. He created the delightful Japanese and Scottish garden, leading down to the estuary of the River Dee at Kirkcudbright. This ancient Burgh, still remains an artists paradise today and is famous for its museums and galleries.

Many other gardens in the area are members of Scotland's Garden Scheme, and are open on selected dates. Bargany, with its magnificent azalea collection, is steeped in local history being one of the former seats of the Kennedy's. For 200 years the Kennedies of Bargany and Cassillis carried on a grievous feud on the moot question of primogenture (they each claimed to be the senior branch of the clan and therefore able to claim the title 'Chief'or 'Head of Clan'). The actual position seems to be that of Bargany but the Cassillis Kennedy history tells a different story! The Kennedies owned Bargany from, at latest, 1455 (when a crown charter of the lands was granted in favour of Thomas Kennedy of Ardstinchar and Kirkoswald and the first of Bargany). His son, Gilbert was in Parliament, and his son Thomas was in the Scottish parliament. In 1601, Gilbert Kennedy, of Bargany and Ardstinchar, was killed by the Earl of Cassillis at Pennyglen, he was returning from a trip to Ayr, with just a small bodyguard, when they were attacked by John Kennedy, the fifth Earl of Cassillis, and a party of 200 men. Gilbert's brother, Thomas of Drummerchie, avenged his brother's death by killing Sir Thomas Kennedy of Cassillis, at St. Leonards Chapel, Ayr, in 1602. Gilbert Kennedy of Bargany, who died at the age of 25, was interred by his wife Janet Stewart, in a Mausoleum behind the old church in Ballantrae where Gilbert and she later joined him. They had three children, two of whom died in infancy, and Thomas, their son, born in 1597, was the last of the Bargany Kennedies.

As there was no heir, in 1631 the Bargany Estate was sold to Sir John Hamilton of Letterick who was granted the Charter of Bargany. He was a bastard son of John 1st Marquess of Hamilton who had been legitimised under the Great Seal in 1600, and was therefore the founder of the family of Hamilton's at Bargany. He was succeeded by his son , John, who was created Lord Bargany by King Charles 1st about 1641. In 1736, James Hamilton, fourth Lord of Bargany, and great, great, grandson of Sir John, died unmarried, the peerage lapsed, and a competition for the Bargany estate arose (known as the first Bargany Cause). This went to the House of Lords, who finally decided on John Dalrymple , the second son of Joanna Hamilton (granddaughter of the 2nd Lord Bargany. Johanna Hamilton had married Sir Robert Dalrymple of Castleton , eldest son of Sir Hew Dalrymple of North Berwick , Lord President of the Court of Session).

In the 18th and 19th centuries there was a great movement towards landscaping grounds and gardens. John Hamilton of Bargany (1715-1796) was a great benefactor of Bargany in many ways, beginning the landscaping of the park lands around the house. He employed William Adam and William Bouchart , both landscape gardeners. In about 1725, John Hamilton employed George Robertson who landscaped round a series of small ponds above which a bowling green was laid out overlooking the ponds.

John Hamilton , although twice married, failed to produce an heir, so on his death he was briefly succeeded by nephew, Sir Hew Dalrymple 3rd Bart of North Berwick. He died at Bargany in 1800 and the estate passed to his son , Hew Dalrymple , who took the additional name of Hamilton , so he became Sir Hew Dalrymple-Hamilton 4th Bart of North Berwick and Bargany. Sir Hew had grand ideas for the Bargany estate and plans were drawn up by William Gilpin, but never implemented. He had roads and bridges built on the estate and began work on the Walled Garden.

In 1822, Henrietta, Sir Hew's only child, married Augustin 3rd Duc de Coigny, who principally lived in Paris. On her father's death she succeeded to the Bargany Estate whilst the Baronetcy and the North Berwick estate passed to Sir Hew's younger brother , John Dalrymple. Henrietta made infrequent visits to Bargany , but they still made considerable alterations to the house and gardens. Other notable gardeners were Thomas White Junior; and later, about 1833, Mr Hay who laid out the formal walled garden and Pineapple House with charming oval entrances (just the foundations remain). There were hot houses heated by coal from Sir Hew Dalrymple Hamilton's own coal mine. The centre of the walled garden is laid down to grass for the farm, but could be returned to garden any day and there are many special trees within the rest of the area, and a Spring Border Garden. In 1826 William Gilpin was employed to make a final plan for the park lands and he formed the present pond from the small ones.

The Bargany and Stair estates became linked when Louisa, daughter of Henrietta, Duchesse de Coigny, married John Hamilton-Dalrymple, and he became the Earl of Stair on his father's death. At this time Lochinch Castle, near Stranraer, became their main residence, Bargany being only used for winter shoots thus became rather neglected, until North de Coigny Dalrymple (Louisa's second son) inherited it on his mother's death. He assumed the additional surname, Hamilton at this time.

The Woodland Garden round the pond was planted by Colonel Sir North Dalrymple Hamilton, along with the rock garden, continued, on his death, by his brother, Admiral Sir Frederick Dalrymple Hamilton. His son, Captain North Dalrymple Hamilton and his wife Mary opened the gardens to the public. Mary Dalrymple Hamilton catalogued all the trees and produced the book 'As Lovely as a Tree', from which much of this information about the garden is taken — a lovely book with great detail about the garden and trees. The present owners, her son John and his wife Sally-Anne Dalrymple Hamilton, are restoring and reconstructing the garden. The bowling green is considered to be one of the oldest in Scotland, built on a bed of ash and bordered by the Eagles brought from Paris by the Duc de Coigny. The garden is famous for its giant leaved rhododendrons, daffodils, embothriums, cercidiphyllum japonicum (katsura), ginkgo biloba (maidenhair), liriodendron tulipifera, acer rufinerve (snake bark maple), taxodium disticchum (swamp cyprus), and collection of lime trees. It is open on Saturday, Sunday and Mondays in May.

May produces lush vegetation, it is a busy time for all gardeners and anything that has not already been planted needs to be! Interesting salads are sprouting and the garden begins to yield its fare.

Caesar salad with avocado and Marrbury smoked chicken

This is a great favourite from our days overseas and now very in vogue in this country. Serves 4:

> A selection of salad leaves including 2 mini gem cos lettuce, lollo rosso, rocket , young spinach leaves etc.
> 1 - Smoked Chicken Breast (ours is from Marrbury Smokehouse)
> 6 tblspn. freshly grated parmesan cheese
> 4 tblspn extra virgin olive oil
> maldon salt
> freshly ground black pepper
> 1 tblspn white wine vinegar
> 1 tblspn lemon juice
> 3 spring onions finely chopped
> 1 tblspn. finely chopped parsley
> 2 fat cloves of garlic
> croutons (made from 2 slices of fresh white bread or a scottish morning roll)
> olive oil to toss the croutons in
> 1 tin or jar of anchovies
> 2 avocados
> 2 softly boiled eggs

- Firstly make the croutons by removing the crusts and cutting into cubes.
- Finely chop 1 clove of garlic and toss in 2 tblspn olive oil with the croutons. Bake in a pre-set oven 160C. for 20 mins. until crisp (these can be prepared ahead of time).
- Wash the salad leaves and dry in a crisper. Wrap in a damp tea towel until needed.
- Boil the eggs for about 8-10 mins.
- Thinly slice the chicken into small pieces.
- Peel the eggs and cut into quarters.
- In a large salad bowl mix together freshly grated parmesan cheese, extra virgin olive oil, seasoning, lemon juice , white wine vinegar, half the anchovies - very finely chopped, finely chopped garlic clove, chopped spring onions and the parsley. (Parsley helps to digest garlic and helps to prevent the pungent smell on your breath!).
- Just before serving add chopped avocado to the dressing, reserving some slices for garnish. Also add most of the chicken , but keep some for garnish.
- When ready to serve, tear up the salad leaves into bite size pieces and toss in the dressing with half the croutons. Toss really well and pile into small bowls , which can then be upturned onto the centre of a large plate.
- Arrange the garnish around the plate - the eggs, chicken, croutons and some thin slithers of freshly sliced parmesan.
- Carefully remove the bowl.
- Finely garnish the salad with the remaining anchovies, crossed on the top.

Fresh Halibut with Sorrel Sauce

Halibut is often farmed these days in Iceland and Canada, which helps to preserve fish stocks in the sea. It is very suited to farming, as it just likes to lie at the bottom of the sea getting fatter! Large fish 3-10kilos (5-20lbs), provide lovely fillets with a firm delicate flavour. Pieronis supply the halibut filleted, which I then cut into suitable portions.

- Toss in melted butter, squeeze the juice of a fresh lime over them, then press on seasoned breadcrumbs. They are then ready to bake in a pre-heated oven 200C. for 7 minutes until firm to touch.

Fresh sorrel, abundant in the garden in May, has a sharp taste to complement the fish. Sorrel is a herb, which thrives in poor soil and is often the first herb to 'show it's face' in the early spring. It needs to be kept well picked, so that there is a plentiful supply of new leaves and to prevent it from going to seed. Protect from slugs.

Sorrel sauce :

> 150 ml (5floz) marinated vegetable stock - see page 91
> 150 ml (5floz) double cream
> fresh lime juice
> a handful of fresh sorrel leaves

- Reduce the marinated vegetable stock to 1-2tblspn. Add any juices from the halibut and reduce again if necessary. Add the cream and reheat gently to boiling point, stirring. If the sauce is too thin add some freshly squeezed lime juice, but do not boil again. Add the freshly chopped sorrel (reserving some for garnish) and serve immediately. Sorrel discolours on cooking, so do not add it until the last minute.

Mousseline of Spinach

> 225g (8oz) of cooked spinach (wash leaves well and tear off the stalks-steam for 5 minutes until cooked, refresh in cold water- press out excess liquid)
> salt, pepper and nutmeg
> 2 eggs

- Place spinach, eggs and the seasoning in a liquidiser/processor and blend for 30 seconds.
- Line ramekins or moulds with overlapping cling film; ¾ fill with spinach mixture, seal with the cling to prevent the water getting into the mousseline. Steam for 7 minutes on high. Turn out and serve as a garnish to the halibut.

Pommes de Terre Forestière

650g (1½lb)potatoes scrubbed or peeled
1 small onion
4 large button mushrooms sliced thinly
25g(1oz) butter
1 tblspn sunflower oil fresh parsley
seasoning

- Cube the potatoes into 2-3cm. cubes (½ in.) . Cover with water and bring to the boil. Drain and shake dry in a colander. Meanwhile melt the butter and oil, add the onion and mushrooms to the pan- toss well. Add the potatoes, shake the pan until well mixed to prevent sticking, and sauté , tossing regularly. Finish in the oven 200c. until crisp. The time will depend on how long they are sautéed for. Once the potatoes are mixed with the onions and mushrooms , they can be completely cooked in the oven for 30-40 minutes until crisp - tossing from time to time. To serve: season well and mix in the finely chopped parsley.

Broad Beans

There are lovely tender small, varieties of broad beans to grow these days. I grow a variety called 'Sterio' or ' Jade' . They freeze well and, other than spinach and peas, are the only vegetable I freeze. Grown in pots undercover, in February and transplanted out in early April, they will be ready to harvest from late May. Sown in succession, tender young beans can be harvested all summer.

- Shell the beans from their pods and rinse.
- Like any vegetable, freshly picked from the garden, just steam for a few minutes and serve.

Brandy Snap Cones filled with Rhubarb Fool served with rhubarb and ginger sauce.

40g (1½oz) sugar   40g (1½oz) golden syrup
40g (1½oz) butter   40g (1½oz) plain flour
½ tspn. ginger   1 tblspn. brandy
1 tblspn. lemon juice

- Pre-heat the oven 170C.
- Melt the butter, sugar and syrup slowly together, until bubbling.
- Sift the flour and ginger into the mixture and stir well.
- Stir in the brandy and lemon juice.
- Drop a meagre level tablespoon onto a baking sheet lined with non stick baking parchment - about 4 to each baking sheet, they spread in the oven. Bake in preheated oven for 7-10 minutes until brown and bubbly . Remove from the oven and leave to cool slightly until JUST firm enough to handle - this is a very exact science! Shape around a cream horn cone. Place on cooling rack until firm - just minutes, then remove the mould. Keep in an air tight container once cold. Continue until all the mixture is used up. They will freeze in an airtight container - do not leave out in the air as they will go soft quickly.

For the rhubarb fool and sauce:

350g (12oz) rhubarb
40g (1½ oz) sugar
200g (7oz) mascaponi or crème fraiche
2 tblspn. green ginger wine
mint leaves or strawberries to garnish

- Wash and slice the rhubarb, then simmer with the sugar, until tender.
- Strain off the excess juice and reserve for the sauce, then rub the remaining rhubarb through a sieve or liquidise until smooth. Cool. Mix some of the puree into the reserved juice with the green ginger wine to make a pouring sauce.
- Beat or blend the remaining puree into the mascaponi or crème fraiche until thick. Beat until the fool just holds its shape.
- Chill.
- To serve fill 2 cones with rhubarb fool mixture and arrange on a plate. Pour around a little of the sauce and garnish with mint leaves and strawberries.

Rhubarb is the earliest 'fruit' (botanically a vegetable) to mature. It should be picked young, before it becomes too acidic, and can be frozen, raw, sliced and tossed on a little sugar, ready for use in compotes, fruit fools and crumbles. It is equally useful for savoury sauces for duck and oily fish.

St.Veran, Domaine Corsin, Maconnais is a delightful wine to complement the halibut.

'The tiny village of Davaye near Macon, southern Burgundy, is the source for this ripe, rounded Chardonnay with it's satisfying, buttery edge - achieved, surprisingly, without resource to new oak. A gem of a wine from the hugely talented Corsin brothers, whose enthusiasm and dedication is matched only by there growing reputation for quality.'

June

Azaleas
(*Watercolour*)
Susan Crosthwaite

Menu:

Fresh Asparagus with a Light Butter Sauce
Fresh Salmon Baked with Lime and Green
Peppercorns, served with Gooseberry and Dill Cream
New Ayrshire Epicure Potatoes
Mange Tout and Early Summer Broccoli
Strawberry Shortcakes with Strawberry and
Elderflower Sauce

JUNE

The rhododendrons and azaleas provide spectacular colour and scent in the shrubbery whilst Mecanopsis - the Himalayan blue poppy with it's dreamlike beauty is one of the finest border perennials in bloom in June. Logan Botanical gardens has a particularly impressive Mecanopsis Boarder. My favourite garden, at this time, is Castle Kennedy and Lochinch garden set in a magnificent 75 acres of outstanding natural beauty. Situated on a peninsula between two beautiful lochs, the garden offers the visitor a choice of walks through the avenues and along the terraces amongst its internationally famous species of azaleas, rhododendrons, magnolias and embothriums.

The Earls of Stair are descended from the historic Scottish family Dalrymple. The Barony of Dalrymple was created in the 13th century, on the NE border of Carrick. Midway through the following century the Barony passed to John Kennedy de Dunure, the ancestor of both the Bargany and Cassillis Kennedies. Today the principle proprietor is the Marquis of Ailsa, scion of the Cassillis branch and chief of the Clan Kennedy .

The Earl of Stair owns Castle Kennedy and Lochinch Castle, in Wigtownshire. In 1601, Gilbert Kennedy of Knockdaw (a castle at Lendalfoot) supported his kinsman Gilbert Kennedy of Bargany when the latter was slain by the 5th Earl of Cassillis- John Kennedy and his party - at Pennyglen near Maybole. Gilbert of Knockdaw's daughter married James Dalrymple of Stair (born in the village of Barr); James's brother, Thomas Dalrymple, was sent to sort out the feuding Kennedies by the King. He was captured by the 5th Earl of Cassillis - John Kennedy - and taken to Craigneil castle at Colmonell, and executed. As a consequence the King confiscated all the Kennedy lands near Stranraer at Castle Kennedy and they were granted to the Dalrymples of Stair, where Sir James Dalrymple became the first Dalrymple to own land in Wigtownshire.

Sir James was a distinguished lawyer whose books on law still form the basis of Scottish law today. He was created 1st Viscount Stair by William III and was succeeded by his son who became the Secretary of State for Scotland in 1691 and created the 1st Earl of Stair in 1704. The second Earl of Stair was a famous military commander who became a Field Marshal . He was appointed to the Court of France as British Ambassador and it was on one of his returns home, from France, that he arrived to find his home in flames. The staff had been airing the bedding in front of open fires!! The family resided at Culhorn, until Lochinch Castle was completed in 1867 to replace Castle Kennedy which was destroyed by the fire in 1716.

A great horticulturist, inspired by the gardens at Versailles, the Field Marshal laid out the grounds around Castle Kennedy in 1730.

The work was done by the men and horses of the Royal Scots Greys and Enniskillen Fusiliers who were stationed in the area to oppose the Covenanters. It is believed that the Field Marshal secretly sympathised with the Covenanters, (as a result of which he had to spend some time in exile), and so found employment for the soldiers in building the terracing and the gardens.

The two houses of Bargany and Stair were linked when John Hamilton Dalrymple married Louisa de Franquetot, the elder daughter of the Duc and Duchesse de Coigny of Bargany. He became the 10th Earl of Stair, on his father's death and Bargany became a winter shooting home during this time. Their principle residence became Lochinch Castle. Bargany became a separate estate when it was left to Louisa's second son, North de Coigny Dalrymple.

The gardens contain fine specimens of trees and rhododendrons that might not flourish in other parts of the Scotland. The Gulf Stream Drift provide climatic conditions peculiar to certain parts of the west coast of Scotland. Rhododendrons grown from seed brought by Sir Joseph Hooker from the Himalayas over 100 years ago are still found in the gardens today. Some of the Beech trees on the loch shore were planted by the second Earl of Stair and are over 250 years old.

Lady Stair (nee Bowes-Lyon and cousin of the Queen), mother of the present Earl, takes a great interest in the gardens and raises many of the plants and shrubs herself. She can often be seen walking with her Labradors or working in the garden and always has time to discuss the latter.

Fresh Asparagus with a light butter sauce

I have tried for years to grow asparagus, but have decided that it is just too wet in this part of the world!

- Remove any woody stems and steam for 5-7 minutes, depending on the thickness of the stems. Serve 6-8 asparagus stem per person.

For the light butter sauce:

150 m l (¼pt.) marinated vegetable stock - see page 91
55g (2oz) butter
75ml (2½ fl.oz) single cream
lemon juice

- Reduce the marinated vegetable stock to 1tblspn. Beat in the butter with a hand beater whist still on a very gentle heat or in a double saucepan. When thick stir in the cream. Reheat but do not boil.
- Add a squeeze of lemon juice and serve around the asparagus.

Fresh salmon baked with lime and green peppercorns with Gooseberry and Dill cream

Fresh salmon is still very popular in spite of it's abundance from the Scottish Salmon farms. I do not cook it very often for guests unless we acquire some wild salmon from the River Stinchar. It is now illegal to buy 'rod caught' salmon.

Salmon fishing has deteriorated over the years that we have lived at Cosses. The Duke of Wellington from the Knockdolian Estates used to allow salmon to be netted in the mouth of the River Stinchar, and wild Salmon were always plentiful in the summer. This is no longer practiced because of dwindling stocks. Blame has been laid at the seals door, as the huge number of seals in this area (always seen basking in Lendlefoot Bay), maim and eat many salmon.

Also the decline is due to todays farming conditions and forestry patterns; i.e. farmers drain the lands so that there is rapid run off causing burns and rivers to spate, washing away salmon eggs, rather than the slow seeping sponge effect of undrained land in days gone by enabling burns and rivers to gradually rise and fall! Also the acidity of the run off from the coniferous forestry over the last 50 years , does not provide ideal breeding conditions for salmon. The main problem is at sea, pollution from fish farming and over fishing by trawlers.

We try to serve wild salmon in preference to farmed, and wild sea bass or hake can be substituted in this recipe for salmon . But ultimately it is the way fish is cooked that is important. I serve fillets of fish (a good fish monger will do this for you), as very few people like to deal with bones.

- Melt a little butter in a baking tin (a metal container heats faster to cook the fish faster), place the fillets of fish in the tin and brush with the butter. Squeeze on the juice of a lime.
- Crush green pepper corns (milder and sweeter than black or white and especially suitable for fish), in a pestle and mortar, or with the end of a rolling pin, and sprinkle over the fish. The fish will only take 5-7 minutes to cook (depending on the thickness of the fillet) - and 2 minutes resting time, in a preheated oven 200C.

Meanwhile make the gooseberry and dill cream

Allow 15g (½oz) gooseberries per person
15g (½oz) butter per person
single cream
chopped or snipped dill

- Gently cook the gooseberries in the butter squashing them with a wooden spoon. When very soft stir in enough single cream to make a coating sauce. Stir in the chopped dill to taste. Serve around the salmon with fresh lime and dill to garnish.

Epicure Potatoes

Epicure potatoes are traditionally grown in this part of Ayrshire. The sandy soils along the coastline warm quickly in the winter sun and are well drained compared to our loamy soils further inland. They are sown very early in December, January and February during mild dry spells of weather and raised under plastic sheeting until risks of frost are past. Consequently, they are ready from May onwards. They are sold direct from farms as well as local shops, Ayr farmer's market (the first Saturday morning of each month). Dowhill farm shop and restaurant started by just selling roadside home-grown potatoes, and developed its farm shop with local produce and home baking. It now incorporates a restaurant serving morning coffees, lunches, afternoon teas and high teas overlooking the Firth of Clyde, Ailsa Craig and Arran. Traffic to and from the Irish Ferries stop to pick up their supply of freshly dug famous early Ayrshire epicure potatoes. They are slightly knobbly so need to be hosed as soon as they are dug; and are slightly sweet therefore are the perfect complement to fish and lamb.

- Depending on size and freshness, steam for 10 to 20 minutes until just tender. Serve with a little butter and snipped chives.
- By the middle of June my first early potatoes are ready, so it becomes very easy to dig up and wash the days requirements.
- Pick the first mange tout and steam for 4-5 minutes. Serve immediately.
- Pick early summer broccoli and also steam for 4-5 minutes and serve, the vegetables should be just cooked but not soft.

Gooseberries, elderflowers, and strawberries all mature in June. Elderflowers are very attractive as a garnish and have a wonderful fragrance. There flavour enhances both strawberries and gooseberries. The flower is in bloom for about a month and is best preserved in syrup (see page 92), which can be frozen and used throughout the year.

To freeze gooseberries pick and pack into punnets and freeze. Wash and trim them whilst still frozen, when you want to use them. They are perfect from the freezer for sauces, fools, crumbles, etc.

I open freeze strawberries, when there is a glut, to use in soufflés, summer puddings and sauces etc. Strawberries are at their best freshly picked, so this most delicious, pretty dessert features quite a lot in June!

Strawberry Shortcakes

Make the shortcakes which will keep well in a tin, or freeze.

> 280g (10oz) plain flour
> 2 tblspn ground rice
> 55g (2oz) icing sugar
> 225g (8oz) scottish unsalted butter

- Sieve the dry ingredients into a bowl. Chop the butter into dice.
- With a K beater in the Kenwood on slow, mix until all the ingredients come together as a dough. Gather together in a ball and on a floured work surface, carefully roll thinly. Cut out shapes with a large fluted (flower) shaped cutter - Tupperware do a perfect size in their set- and place on a baking sheet lined with baking parchment. Bake in a preheated oven 160C for about 10 minutes until just pale golden. Cool slightly, and carefully remove

onto a cooling rack with a spatula. Keep in a sealed container until required.

- Line 4 chinese soup dishes- smaller than rice dishes (the perfect shape for this dessert and cheaply acquired from a chinese supermarket) with cling film, overlapping the edges.
- Slice large strawberries, put one in the bottom of each dish and arrange the other slices, point to the centre, around the side of the dish. Reserve some strawberry slices for the top. Meanwhile chop some strawberries roughly, and fold into crème fraiche with vanilla sugar to taste (made by storing vanilla pods in a jar of sugar - the flavour infuses into the sugar). Divide between the strawberry lined dishes, top with the remaining slices, and fold over the overlapping cling film. Refrigerate until needed.
- To serve: place a shortcake in the middle of each plate. Open the cling film and carefully turn out the strawberry dessert into the centre of the shortcake . Drizzle a little strawberry and elderflower sauce around the edge.
- To make the sauce: Puree strawberries with a little elderflower syrup- see page 92.
- Garnish with elderflowers and strawberries and serve.

Bycos Viognier, Bodegas Vinterra,Lujan De Cuyo, Argentina is the wine suggestion for July's menu:

'A unique climate, careful selection of grapes, modern technology and a team of highly skilled oenologists combine to produce a wine of real distinction. The grapes have been whole bunch pressed with 100% of the wine aged in French oak. Golden straw in colour with green hues, this Viognier Reserve is powerfully aromatic showing lemon, lime, apricot and tropical fruit flavours. It is a perfect example of fruit and oak, combined to produce a young vibrant and unique wine.'

JULY

Cosses Country House & Garden

(Watercolour)
Susan Crosthwaite

Menu:

Courgettes Stuffed with Tomatoes, Shallots and
Peppers, finished with Mornay Sauce
Ballantrae Lobster with Cucumber and
Strawberry Salad
Green Mayonnaise, Cosses New potatoes
Summer Vegetable Salad
Blackcurrant and Redcurrant Brûlée

JULY

The perennial borders dominate this month with magnificent displays in all the gardens . Afternoon tea in the garden at Cosses is always a treat , but especially this month. Logan, Cally gardens (3000 varieties are planted here in 30 borders.), and the walled garden at Culzean are particularly spectacular at this time.

A visit to Culzean is an absolute must for everyone. Perched high on cliffs, above the Firth of Clyde, 100 feet sheer above the sea, Culzean is considered one of Scotland's most impressive stately homes. Several large caves penetrate the cliffs beneath the castle and were probably inhabited by early man in Ayrshire. Culzean is the historic seat of the Marquesses of Ailsa and the Earls of Cassillis. The imposing 18th century mansion, built near the site of a castle named the 'Cove', was designed by Robert Adam and was given to the National Trust for Scotland in 1945, and is now their most visited property.

Culzean Castle was originally built in 1777 for the 10th Earl of Cassillis as a bachelor pad for entertaining his friends. This was done in four stages over a period of 15 years. Firstly a 4 storey L shaped tower house, was built which was 'squared up' and a three storey wing was added with a kitchen block. In 1785 the Earl's wing was demolished and a huge drum tower with rooms on either side was built to form a more unified building where the very impressive circular saloon was created. There was still a damp dark central courtyard in the centre of the building which was utilised in 1787 to form a grand oval staircase. The result unified the whole castle and makes the staircase the central feature rather than an addition - a masterpiece of Adam's design. The building of Culzean must have put a strain on Adam as it did on the Earl. In a letter sent to his banker in 1790, Lord Cassillis wrote, '—I hope my operations will (soon) be at an end for I am really wearied of Building and wish to be at rest.' Meanwhile, Adam the workaholic continued with several commissions, dashing between London and Scotland, and ignoring pains from his ulcer. Culzean was completed in 1792 but the decoration continued until 1795. In March 1792 Adam died of a stomach haemorrhage; Lord Cassillis followed him in December of the same year.

When the castle was given to the National Trust the Kennedy family asked that part of it be given to General Eisenhower for his lifetime to show the gratitude of the Scots to the Supreme Commander of the Allied Forces in Europe. An exhibition illustrates Eisenhower's connections and visits to the castle. The National Trust for Scotland began a full restoration of the castle and grounds in 1972 with advice from the Victoria and Albert Museum and under the helpful eye of Rab Snowden of the Stenhouse Conservation Centre in Edinburgh. The full restoration was carried out in the original manner by the local craftsman Mr Robert Howie of Mauchline.

Outside major restoration of stonework is taking place and includes the Swan Pond Court, the Gas House , the Camellia House, the Castle Court , the Clock Tower Court, the Fountain, the Cat Gates, the Pagoda , the Gazebo and Old Stables, the New Stables, the seaward face of the castle, and most significant of all , the unique Viaduct and ruined Arch. Interpretation and adaptive use of the restored buildings has allowed an Education centre to be created in the Clock Tower Court, and the Gas House exhibitions, explaining it's history as a source of fuel supply to the castle, as well as the historical evolution of gas and it's impact nationally.

In 1996 the grounds became Scotland's first Country Park. The exciting blend of history and the superb natural setting , the regard for conservation and expert management have made this 560 acre estate the most visited National Trust Property. Current management policy is to restructure and re-establish the picturesque landscape, retaining the character of the late 18th century estate. The ranger service, established in 1970, provides a link between the visitor and the park, with a very popular programme of events, films, talks, and guided walks, and a Young Naturalists Club. A list of special events throughout each season including concerts, recitals, fun runs, sheepdog competitions, Shakespeare productions, bands, Scottish country dancing, classic vehicle show, falconry, horse trials and craft and food fares, and a Victorian family Christmas; is available .

The Kennedy family has been associated with the province of Carrick since the end of the 12th century and are descendants of the Lord of Galloway - Fergus Mac dubh Ghael, who had a grandson, Roland, (brother to the Earl of Carrick - Duncan MacDowall). Roland's great, great granddaughter, and heiress was Mary MacDowall de Carrick who married John Kennedy de Dunure, and thus founded the great Kennedy Clan . Mary MacDowall, as the heiress of the third senior branch of the ancient Lords of Galloway, brought many lands and castles of western Galloway, including Ardstinchar (to which Cosses belonged), Lochinch, Loch Ryan and others, into the Kennedy family and explains their sudden rise to power. John Kennedy de Denure was a descendant of Henry Kennedy who was a brother of William the Lion.

John and Mary's eldest son and heir Gilbert, had a son, also Gilbert. This Gilbert married Marion Sandilands of Calder and they had three sons - Gilbert Kennedy of Dunure and Ardstinchar, John Kennedy of Cove (Culzean), and Roland Kennedy of Leffnoll (Loch Ryan). This family of Sir Gilbert and Marion became known as the Bargany branch of the Kennedy family, when Gilbert remarried. There is no record of what happened to Marion Sandilands, or when or where she died; but Gilbert remarried Agnes Maxwell.

By Gilbert's second wife, Agnes Maxwell of Pollok, Gilbert had a family of six sons; Sir James Kennedy of Dunure, Alexander, Hew - killed at the battle of Anjou in 1421, John of Blairquhan, Thomas and David. This family became known as the Kennedies of Cassillis. James Kennedy of Dunure (eldest of this second family) married Mary ,daughter of King Robert111, in 1405. On this royal marriage arrangements were apparently made between King Robert111 and Sir Gilbert Kennedy that the Bargany branch of the family should be disinherited (and declared illegitimate) so that Sir James and the Princess should become heir to his father and his many lands. (It was and is legal to disinherit a person, or persons, but it is not legal to declare a legitimate family 'illegitimate'). So began a feud that was to go on for two centuries. From the time when Sir James Kennedy married the King's daughter, he became 'Chief' of the Clan Kennedy; and from then until this day, the eldest male of the Cassillis Kennedies has been 'Chief of the Kennedy Clan.

As one would expect, the senior (Bargany) branch of the Kennedies violently resented these proceedings. In a quarrel between Bargany - Gilbert, and his half brother , Sir James, in 1408, Sir James was killed. The question remains as to why Gilbert should have killed his half brother and why he did not have to pay the usual penalty? As it happens the Bargany branch died out in 1631 and the estates were acquired by John Hamilton of Letterick. (see Chapter 5).

Gilbert Kennedy (son of James and Princess Mary) became the 1st Lord Kennedy, his son John became the 2nd Lord Kennedy of Turnberry, Girvan Mains and of Cove (Culzean) and his son Sir David Kennedy became the 1st Earl of Cassillis - he was killed at Flodden in 1513. The 2nd Earl of Cassillis - Scots ambassador to England was killed by Sir Hugh Campbell in 1527, and 3rd Earl of Cassillis acquired the Barony of Craigneil in 1557, but was taken prisoner at Solway Moss. The 4th Earl was entitled King of Carrick and fought for Mary Queen of Scots at Langside. The feud continued and John Kennedy 5th Earl of Cassillis (with 200 men), slew Gilbert Kennedy of Bargany and Ardstinchar in 1601, as he was returning from Ayr, with just a small bodyguard, near Pennyglenn, outside Maybole. At the same time John Kennedy was also responsible for the execution of his cousin Thomas Dalrymple (brother of the Earl of Stair), whose only crime was to be a friend of Gilbert of Bargany. The execution took place at Craigneil castle at Colmonell - one of the oldest mediaeval castles in the Stinchar Valley. So great was the power of the Kennedies that :

'Twixt Wigtoun and the toun o' Ayr
Port patrick and the Cruives o' Cree
Nae man need think fur tae bide there
Unless he court wi' Kennedie.'

John, 5th Earl of Cassillis, had no direct heir ,thus John's brother's son, who was a prominent Covenanter (signed Solemn League and Covenant in 1601) became the 6th Earl. The Feud between the Kennedy's became overshadowed by the greater struggle for religious liberty.

John Kennedy, 7th Earl was followed by his grandson of the same name, who left no heir. Consequently Sir Thomas Kennedy of Culzean, by decision of the House of Lords, after a three year court dispute, became the 9th Earl in 1762. He and his brother, who succeeded him in 1776, were active 'improvers' of their estates. Again there were no direct heirs, and the title passed to Captain Archibald Kennedy, Royal Navy of New York. Archibald's son, the 12th Earl, became the 1st Marquess of Ailsa. The 2nd Marquess was killed in a hunting accident, thus the 3rd, Archibald, succeeded at 22, and lived to be 90 years old. After his death in 1938 he was succeeded by each of his three sons in turn. In 1945 the 5th Marquess and the Kennedy family gave the castle and care of the estate to the National Trust for Scotland. David, 7th Marquess of Ailsa and 18th Earl of Cassillis died in 1994 and was succeeded by the present 8th Marquess and 19th Earl, Charles Kennedy. He and his wife Anne, have two children and Kitty their daughter is a keen naturalist, participating in many events at Culzean.

This is a month when there is an abundance of fresh fruit and vegetables and it is wonderful to walk into the kitchen garden and select whatever takes ones fancy - a treat for the senses. I often serve a platter of half a dozen vegetables so that our guests can taste lots of them for themselves.

Courgettes stuffed with tomatoes, shallots and peppers finished with mornay sauce

This is a wonderful vegetable starter. Courgettes are best picked when small as they have more flavour. Serves 4.

25g(1oz) butter	4 small courgettes
3 tomatoes	1 red pepper
2 shallots	1 tsp. paprika
parmesan cheese	300 ml (½ pint) béchamel sauce (see page 91)

- Blanch courgettes by placing them in boiling water and simmering for 1 minute. Refresh in cold water.
- Skin the tomatoes (placing in boiling water for 30 seconds and then plunge into cold water), de-seed and chop.
- Chop the shallots and the red pepper. Along the length of each courgette cut off a thin slice. With a grapefruit knife carefully remove the flesh to make a boat shape. Place on a buttered gratin dish.
- Chop the courgette flesh. Melt the butter and add the shallots then the paprika and cook for 1 minute. Add the pepper and courgette flesh and lastly the tomatoes. Divide the mixture between each courgette boat.
- Make the béchamel sauce adding any juice from the tomato seeds. Stir until thick and smooth. Spoon over the stuffed courgettes and sprinkle with the parmesan cheese. These can be prepared well ahead. Refrigerate when cold if to be kept for any length of time.
- To finish, preheat the oven to 200C. Bake for 10 - 15 minutes until the cheese is golden then serve garnished with parsley or basil.

Ballantrae Lobster

Opposite Ballantrae the gap between Ireland and the Mull of Kintyre allows the Atlantic and its gulf stream to penetrate the rocky shores providing a great breeding ground for lobsters, crabs, prawns and scallops. Ballantrae fishermen have enjoyed this fertile plane for hundreds of years. Today Eric McIllwraith has become a legend in his own lifetime, a name synonymous with the perfect lobster. There is nothing quite like a live shiny black/navy lobster.

- I find that the kindest way to deal with them is to place a very sharp knife through the cross on their head and plunge them into a large pan of boiling water. A good tip is to flavour the water with a bay leaf and a few pepper corns, salt and a little white wine vinegar.
- Bring back to the boil and simmer for 5 minutes, until pink. Cool in the water until required.
- To clean the lobster, break off the claws, then carefully split the body in half and remove the black vein and sack.
- Using a knife carefully lift out the tail meat and rinse out the shell and reserve.
- Return the meat to the opposite shell rounded side up. Using very strong sharp scissors cut open the claws and carefully remove the meat. It should come out in the shape of the claws. Place in the body part of the lobster shell.

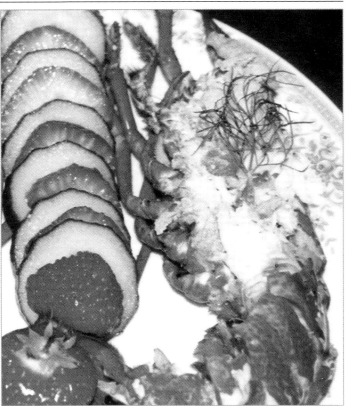

Garnish a plate with salad leaves e.g. lollo rosso lettuce, rocket, sorrel. Place the lobster in the centre garnished with dill, and lemon and cucumber twists.
Serve the mayonnaise separately.

Green mayonnaise

300 ml (½ pint) mayonnaise (see page 92)

- A handful of fresh mixed herbs e.g. sorrel, dill, tarragon, chives, parsley and fennel. Be sparing with the tarragon and fennel as both are dominant flavours.
- Chop finely and add to the mayonnaise with a squeeze of lemon juice and 2 tablespoons of single cream.

Cosses new potatoes

New potatoes freshly dug from the garden just need washing with a fierce hose pipe immediately after digging. I am very partial to Belle de Fontayne, Roseval and Ratte - forming a sequence of new potatoes, and each year I try two or three new varieties.

- When potatoes are so fresh they really only need steaming for 10 - 15 minutes. Toss in a little butter to make them shine and sprinkle with snipped chives.

Strawberry and cucumber salad
Slice strawberries and layer with slices of cucumber. Sprinkle on lots of black pepper and a little dry white wine to serve.

Summer vegetable salad
Take a selection of mange tout, French green beans and broad beans and steam lightly. Refresh in cold water, strain and toss in a little French dressing (see page 92). Serve.

Blackcurrant and Redcurrant Brûlée

The currant bushes are always laden at this time of year and I have a wonderful Mum who loves picking them. She covers herself from head to foot so that the fruit flies don't eat her - sits on an overturned bucket and picks dozens of punnets which go straight into the freezer if they are not immediately made into delicious desserts.

Pick the redcurrants on their stalks and de-stalk when frozen by rolling gently between your hands. Rinse in a colander and they are ready to use as fresh. Blackcurrants are more easily picked off their stalks but again should be washed when frozen before use.

6 medium ramekin dishes	6 tsp. cassis
115g blackcurrants	6 level tsp. sugar
115g redcurrants	3 egg yolks, large
40g(1½oz) vanilla sugar	Demerara sugar

350ml (12fl.oz) double cream (or a mixture of crème frais and single cream or double and single) infused with a vanilla pod.

- Place blackcurrants and redcurrants in each ramekin. Sprinkle with 1 level teaspoon of sugar and 1 teaspoon cassis.

- Infuse the cream with the vanilla pod by heating gently, then scrape the seeds into the cream , by cutting the pod in half , lengthways and scraping the seeds out with the point of a knife.
- In a mixing bowl beat the egg yolks and vanilla sugar until pale and creamy. Then beat in the warm, infused cream . Pour over the currants.
- Place in a bain marie and bake in a preheated oven, 160C, for about 30 minutes until just set, firm on top. They will finish setting in the fridge.
- Refrigerate for at least two hours.
- Sprinkle with demerara sugar and brûlée with a kitchen blow torch or under a very hot grill.
- Refrigerate until needed. Serve with a bunch of redcurrants and a blackcurrant leaf for garnish.

To complement the lobster Chablis premier Cru, 'Montmains', Domaine de Vauroux

From the independent' family run Vauroux estate come this rich, fruity Chablis, a dry and intensely flavoured wine with the lovely mineral 'cut' that sets this style of chardonnay apart from any other Burgundy. Montmains is one of the more highly rated of the premiere Cru ('first growth') vineyards in Chablis, which are themselves a cut above 'straight' Chablis.

August

'Cosses' "Hidden in a valley"

(Watercolour)
Susan Crosthwaite

Menu:

Ballantrae Prawns with Garlic, Spring Onions,
Cream and Arran Malt
Guinea Fowl cooked on a Mirepoix of Vegetables with
Fresh Ginger finished with a Port and Berry Sauce.
Platter of Cosses Summer Vegetables
Czar Plum Tarte Tâtin with Home-made
Vanilla Icecream

AUGUST

From the coastline and hills of Southwest Scotland the distinctive silhouette of the Isle of Arran is never far from view during the long clear days of August. Arran with its rolling, heather clad moorland, and sandy beaches, is a favourite spot for a day trip from Cosses. The ferry crossing from Ardrossan takes one hour and the island, with it's 56 miles of coastline can easily be explored in a day. For a small island, Arran plays a large part in Scottish folklore . There are the stone circles on Machrie Moor with their mysterious aura so evocative of Stonehenge; and it is in a hidden cave at Blackwaterfoot where Robert the Bruce is said to have had that monumental moment when he had his encounter with a spider; before the battle of Glen Trool.

The towering presence of Goatfell Pike dominates the island which boasts numerous walks and climbs, water-sports and seven golf courses.

Brodick Golf Club is a park land course, while Lamlash must be one of the most beautiful courses in the world, overlooking the bay towards the Holy Island. Whiting Bay looks back towards the Ayrshire Hills and Ailsa Craig, whilst Blackwaterfoot (or Shiskine) Golf Club is an exceptional course even though it only has 12 holes. Machrie and Lochranza are relatively simple 9 hole courses, but Corrie has 9 challenging holes surrounded by mountains which give the impression of playing into the teeth of a monster.

Brodick Castle, an imposing building, overlooks the sea on the site of a fortress originally built by the Vikings. Over the years the castle has been destroyed and rebuilt by the many warring factions in struggles for power which make it the nations most battle scarred stronghold. Only during the 19th century did it develop into the residence of the Dukes of Hamilton. Now administered by the National Trust for Scotland, it is a treasury of porcelain and silverware, works by Watteau, Herring, and Vrank, sketches by Gainsborough and a watercolour by Turner. The rooms are adorned with furniture from all around the world, Dutch marquetry tables, Japanese carvings and Chinese porcelain. The castle overlooks 65 acres of woodland and garden with breathtaking displays of rhododendrons and magnolias, formal walled garden and follies such as the Bavarian summerhouse.

You do not think of Scotland without thinking of whisky, and a visit to Arran would not be complete without a visit to the Distillery! Situated in Lochranza in the north of the island, it is easily recognised by its copper pagodas, where there are regular conducted tours. Robin is a founder member of the distillery thus you will find the single malt amongst Cosses' fine collection.

Another great day out, is to the Isle of Cumbrae - a ten minute ferry ride from Largs. The island is flat and only 11 mile, around its perimeter so cycling is safe and 'the thing to do' for all age groups. Millport, the island's only town, has its own cathedral, Britain's narrowest house, and numerous cycle-hiring shops. The charm of this little town, facing the Isle of Arran is quite unique and a must for any visitor. There are many fascinating geological features, to look out for, including the famous Crocodile and Indian rocks, and lots of sandy bays in which to enjoy a picnic.

August is also the month of Ayr Flower show, held in the lovely woodland setting of Rozelle Park. The show was originally funded by the local authority, but is now organised by the Ayrshire Horticultural Society under the leadership of the former flower show director David Roy. There are exhibits of floral displays, horticultural machinery, handicrafts, amateur exhibits of flowers, fruit and vegetables, honey, wine and begonias- (for which Ayr is famous)- together with craft demonstrations, music, gardeners question time, and entertainers as well as traders of anything associated with gardening. It is my source of sweet pea and delphinium seeds, special plants and herbs, not to mention local produce.

Ballantrae Prawns with garlic, spring onions, cream and Arran Malt

Local Prawns are always a favourite straight from the boats, landed in Girvan harbour . They are tender and delicate in flavour, to clean see December on Prawns.(serves 4)

> 250g (1lb) medium prawns
> 4 large whole prawns for garnish
> 4 slices of fresh white French bread
> 2 cloves of garlic
> bunch of spring onions
> bunch of fresh parsley
> 1 tblspn Arran Malt whisky
> 150 ml (5fl.oz) double cream
> ¼ tspn. cornflour
> 25-50 g butter and 1-2 tblspn sunflower oil.

- Peel the prawns, removing the backbone. Just remove the backbone from the whole prawns.
- Finely chop the garlic, and slice the spring onions.
- Cut the French bread into diagonal slices
- Melt 25g (1oz) of butter and 1 tblspn oil, add half the garlic, and dip the bread into it - to coat, before placing on a baking sheet. Dip the whole prawns into the butter and oil. then bake with the bread, in a pre-set oven 180C. for 5 minutes.
- Meanwhile add the remaining butter and oil, gently cook the remaining garlic and spring onions for a minute, turn up the heat, add the prawns and cook for 2 minutes.
- Mix the whisky, cream and cornflour together and pour over the remaining prawns and stir gently until just bubbling.
- Finely chop the parsley - reserving some for garnish, and stir into the prawn mixture. Serve immediately on warm plates, the croûte in the centre, the prawn mixture, and a whole prawn to garnish, finishing with some flat leaved parsley.

Guinea Fowl cooked on a mirepoix of vegetables with fresh ginger finished with a port and berry sauce.

Guinea Fowl makes a lovely change to chicken, having a stronger flavour. It is supplied locally by Braehead Foods.

> 1 tbspn oil
> 25g (1oz) butter
> 4 suprêmes of guinea fowl or chicken breasts
> 1 carrot 1 onion 2 mushrooms — finely sliced
> small piece of ginger very finely chopped
> small wineglass of port
> 300ml demi-glace sauce see page 91
> 1 tspn red currant jelly
> 175 g blackberries , blackcurrants and raspberries
> watercress to garnish

- Brown the guinea fowl in the butter and oil in a flame proof casserole. Set aside.
- Soften the onion, carrot and mushroom in the remaining oil with the finely chopped ginger. Arrange the guinea fowl on the vegetable mirepoix, pour over the port, cover the casserole and place in a preheated oven 180c. for one hour.
- Remove the guinea fowl and keep warm. Strain the sauce and add the redcurrant jelly and demi glace sauce to the port sauce. Reheat and reduce if necessary. Just before serving stir in the berries.
- Diagonally carve the suprêmes into 4 or 5 thick slices and arrange on warm plates with some of the sauce and berries.
- Garnish with watercress and serve.

This is the time of year when all the summer vegetables are available in the garden, so a platter of several is very appealing and attractive to serve for dinner. The potatoes just need digging up, hosing -to wash- and they are ready to steam. Roseval is one of the varieties that I grow, - it is pink, kidney shaped, and produces an abundance of small tubers, which are a paler colour on cooking, thus look very attractive. A choice of young tender carrots, mange tout, french beans, broad beans, beetroot, yellow and green courgettes, broccoli, cauliflower, spinach and swiss chard.

Choose a variety of textures and colour which will look good on the platter. The beetroot has to be scrubbed and boiled for 30 minutes. Peel under cold running water whilst still hot, a variety of colours can be grown and they make a super garnish. All the other vegetables can be steamed, the potatoes 15 -20 minutes, the carrots 7-10 minutes, the other vegetables about 4-5 minutes - all until just cooked.

The vegetables are then lined up on a large platter in alternating colours and shapes. Finish with a little butter on the potatoes.

Plum Tart Tatin with Home-made Vanilla Ice cream

The Czar plum tree ripens first in August, followed by the Victoria in September.

Like gooseberries, the plums freeze well, just washed, dried and in plastic bags. They are great for compots, crumbles and tarts as well as for savoury sauces .

For pastry:

175g (6oz) plain flour
1 tblspn sugar
grated rind of a lemon
100g (3½oz) butter
1 egg yolk
2 tblspn cold water

- Sift the flour into a bowl with the sugar. Chop up the butter and rub into the flour (with a K beater) until it resembles breadcrumbs. Add the finely chopped lemon rind. (A zester is a wonderful gadget for pearing rind of citrus fruit.) Mix the egg yolk with the cold water and add to the mixture to make a dough. Do not over mix at this stage. Bring together, wrap in cling film and chill for half an hour.

For the Plums:

700g (1½lb plums) Halved and stoned
55g (2oz) butter
55g (2oz) sugar
4 cloves
5 cm cinnamon stick
½ glass of red wine

- In a heavy frying pan, melt the butter and add the sugar, cloves and cinnamon stick and cook stirring for 1-2 minutes, until the sugar starts to brown. Add ½ glass of red wine, the plums and cook over a high heat until the juices begin to run, stirring carefully.
- Remove the plums and arrange in a large flan dish, or individual dishes, cut side up. Remove the cloves and cinnamon.
- Pour over the plum juices (reduced slightly if necessary). Leave to cool.
- Roll out the pastry to fit the dishes and lightly lay on top of the plums, prick the pastry to allow the steam to escape. Chill for at least half an hour, or until needed.
- Pre-set the oven 200C. and bake for 20 minutes until the pastry is golden.
- Cool for 5 minutes, then carefully invert and turn out onto a large flat plate.
- Serve with scoops of vanilla ice-cream - see page 94, and garnish with nasturtium flowers.

Nasturtium flowers make wonderful garnishes for desserts and salads. They taste of cucumbers.

Pick and rinse, and keep in a glass of water until required.

Unoaked Chardonnay Cantine Settesoli (Sicily), Italy is the wine to complement the Prawns and the Guinea Fowl:

'From the renowned Settesoli co-operative in Manfi which uses centuries of local wine making tradition, combined with the latest technical advances, to give a refreshingly modern white. Ripe green apple, macadamia nuts, and honey aromas precede a soft, rich palate with a fat, round, satisfying finish.'

September

Dusk falls on Newbridge in the centre of Ayr

(Watercolour)
Susan Crosthwaite

Menu:

Wild Mushroom and Tobermory Cheddar Feuilleté
Fillet of Locally Reared Beef (cooked to taste) and
served with a Whisky, Dijon, Cream Sauce
Château Potatoes
Cosses Mixed Salad with French Dressing
Baked Autumn Bliss Raspberry Creams

September

R oman records refer to the existence of a highway from southern Galloway to Ayr and the north; and the ancient ford at the mouth of the River Ayr, must have existed from early Pictish days.

Dalquharran, a castle built by the Cassillis Kennedies, 1/2 mile north of New Dailly village, was apparently a huge Pictish burial ground. There was a Pictish King's Cairn at Drummochreen to the north east of the castle, and a Pictish Fortress on Hadyards Hill, 2 miles south of the castle. For miles around the site, Pictish remains and Gaelic names indicate an early civilisation in this area, but much of the evidence has been lost in the mists of antiquity, and the stones been used to build houses. Two and a half miles NE of New Dailly lies the estate of Kilkerran, where many Pictish remains have been found, including a chaldron of the bronze age, parts of Bronze swords, knives and stone chisels. This estate has been in the Fergusson family since the reign of Robert the Bruce. Sir Charles Fergusson of Kilkerran is one of the few scions of noble families who today, retain and occupy lands held by their family in continuous succession for over 600 years. The family is descended from a Fergus, who obtained a charter of these lands from King Robert the Bruce, and it is very probable that he was a grandson, or great grandson of Fergus MacDowall, Lord of Galloway, as was Robert the Bruce. Brigadier Bernard Fergusson distinguished himself under General Stillwell in Burma in the Second World War, and is the author of 'Beyond the Chindwin' - a story of amazing hazards and adventure.

Sir William Wallace, born in 1270, was the younger son of Sir Malcolm Wallace of Elderslie, Renfrewshire, and Margaret Jean, daughter of Sir Reynold Crawford, sheriff of Ayr. William married Marion Bradfute, the heiress of Lamington, who was put to death by the English at Lanark in 1297. In that year William became guardian of Scotland until his execution, in London in 1305. On 18th June 1297 the English invaders organised and carried out a massacre of the leading Scots of Kyle, Cunninghame and Carrick, in the Barns of Ayr. Wallace was warned by his niece, thus he did not attend the 'Justice-air'- the meeting arranged in the Barns (in Wellington Square). All who attended were massacred. In Laglane Wood a rendezvous was organised for a vengeance party and whilst the murderers were celebrating their exploits, that evening, Wallace and his party surrounded the Barns and set them on fire, where everyone of the murderers perished, either in the flames or at the exits guarded by the avenging Scots. Wallace defied the English King Edward 1st and after clearing Glasgow of the invaders, he defeated Edward's army at Scone , and on September 11th, 1297, Wallace defeated the English at Stirling Bridge.

In May 1305 Wallace was betrayed and captured by Sir John Monteith who is said to have handed him over to Edward. Wallace was carried through the streets of London on 22nd August and tried at Westminster by special commission, where he was convicted of treason and rebellion and was executed on 23rd August 1305. He was dragged by horses through the streets of London to the gallows in Smithfield. After being hanged for a very short time, he was cut down and whilst still breathing, his bowels were torn out and burned. Thereafter, his body was beheaded and quartered, his head was fixed on a pole on London Bridge and his quarters were sent to Stirling, Berwick, Perth and Aberdeen, where they were exhibited as warnings to rebellious Scots! The ghastly episode effected a purpose — it set aflame the torch of freedom for Scotland. This freedom was attained nine years later by Robert the Bruce at Bannockburn on 24th June 1314. On 26th April 1315 the Scottish Parliament met in Ayr at Saint John's Tower and confirmed the succession to the Scots crown. St. John's Tower is open to the public by arrangement.

Ayr is the largest town on the coast, and remains a traditional seaside town, which has been popular since the railway age with its plush Victorian Villas and old town houses like Loudoun Hall. It is famous as the birthplace of Robert Burns - see page 13. Scotland's premiere racecourse is in Ayr with races spread throughout the year, including the Scottish Grand National in April and Ayr Gold Cup in September.

The only sea going paddle steamer, the Waverly, leaves from Ayr (and occasionally Girvan) to cruise around the beautiful islands and sea lochs of the Firth of Clyde.

With amenities like the famous Gaiety Theatre, Civic and Borderline theatres, many high street stores, Alex Begg's cashmere outlet, and numerous restaurants and bars, Ayr has plenty to offer the visitor.

Ayrshire, of course is famous for its golf courses and the introduction of the Ayrshire golf classics, (spring summer and autumn) four days golf at some of Scotland's finest courses including Turnberry, Bogside -near Irvine, Barassie - near Troon and Bellisle in Ayr (2001).

Prestwick Golf Club is very high on many a golfers wish list, the 'quirky dinosaur' might not be up to the modern championship standards, but it is one of it's treasures. The first Open Championship came to Prestwick on October 17th 1860, and what began as a simple competition on the 12 hole course laid out by Tom Morris between eight of Scotland's leading golfers, turned into the most important golf competition in the world. The greatest hole on the course hasn't changed since it's design in 1850, the 17th, with it's blind second shot, its high ridge of dunes and great 'Sahara' bunker in front of the green.

Royal Troon, consisting of the Old and the Portland Courses, lie on an exceptional stretch of links land between Troon and Prestwick. The Old is the Open Championship Course, but the Portland will test even the best players, with it's adroitly placed bunkering and small glossy greens. The Postage Stamp, the Old's course's most famous hole has seen some dreadful scores, as the prevailing side winds, and cavernous bunkers take their toll!

Turnberry offers one of the most superior links courses in the world, with an amazing club house and Colin Montgomerie Links Golf Academy. Tuition packages, prepared by Colin Montgomerie and a team of experts will make sure that you will get the best from your game. There is the Ailsa Course where three open championships have taken place (with much praise), which begins relatively straight forwardly. By the 6th hole the pressure is turned up, with a deceptive par three of over 200 yards - an ego killer in a head wind! The 9th, Bruce's castle, with the famous Turnberry Lighthouse perched on an outcrop of igneous rock, is one of the most photographed in the world. The newly named and upgraded Kintyre course (formally Arran) is now of championship standard with 11 entirely new holes with more undulating greens and fairways and lots of scottish gorse.

For the casual golfer there are courses to suit everyones pace to a tee! Girvan offers a seaside/park land course in two sections which is relatively flat, but the wind can turn this innocuous course into a demon. Seafield is less taxing than its neighbour Belleisle (in Ayr), Prestwick offers simpler courses in St. Cuthberts and St. Nicholas, and in the municipality course Fullarton (in Troon).

For someone who wants more of a challenge Brunston Castle near Girvan will sort the 'men from the boys'. You need to be strong off the tee, but with water, trees and wind all considerably affecting play, you need to have a cool head to come off close to your handicap.

South of Cosses offers some scenic challenging courses, tucked away in the quiet corner of the Southwest, away from the pressures of busy courses. (It is still wise to book, but you can usually choose your time.) - Stranraer - overlooking Loch Ryan, with it's new clubhouse; and Portpatrick (Dunskey) have a keen edge to keep the low handicapper happy. Dunskey is particularly scenic with sheer cliffs and sandy bays visible beneath the rolling headland on which the course is built. Southerness Golf Club, just south of Dumfries, is often voted one of the most difficult courses in the UK, with it's boggy marshes lining the fairways. Newton Stewart is a charming but testing little course, a mixed collection of interesting and sometimes rigorous holes, where accuracy is everything. Wigtownshire County by Glenluce is an ideal venue for a relaxed and unconstrained round, a flat course stretching down to the beach with lovely wide fairways.

This is the month when wild mushrooms are plentiful in the fields and the hillsides. Sometimes the fields are almost white with mushrooms as large as tea plates and I like to pick them small and young, not quite open. I always do a large batch of concentrated soup for the freezer. The following recipe is a lovely combination of wild mushrooms and mature cheddar cheese.

Wild Mushroom and Tobermory Cheddar Feuillete

Ready rolled sheet of puff pastry
Grated parmesan cheese
Paprika Pepper
350g (12oz) wild mushrooms sliced
85 g 3oz grated Tobermory cheddar
300ml (½ pt) béchamel sauce see page 91
salad garnish

- Lay out the puff pastry and sprinkle grated parmesan cheese and paprika pepper over it. Cut it into rectangles about 12 cm x 6 cm. Place on a baking sheet and chill for 10 minutes, before placing in a pre-heated oven 210C. for 5 minutes until well risen and golden.
- Meanwhile cook the béchamel sauce stirring all the time.
- Stir in the grated Tobermory cheese.
- At the same time melt the butter over a medium heat, add the mushrooms and fry briskly, tossing well until cooked.
- Slice the Feuillete horizontally in half and place on a warm plate.
- Gently fold the mushrooms into the cheese sauce and divide between the Feuillete bases. Top with the pastry lid and garnish with salad leaves and cherry tomatoes and serve.

Fillet of Locally Reared Beef (cooked to taste) and served with Whisky, Dijon, Cream Sauce

Fillet of beef is without doubt the best cut of beef for steaks and fast cooking . The length of time that the beef is hung, is crucial in producing a tender, tasty steak - thus knowing your butcher well is a great advantage. Order your fillet steaks in advance - if you can - to allow time for hanging.

4 x 175g (6oz) fillet steaks
30g butter
freshly ground black pepper
bunch of spring onions
2 tblspn whisky
1 tblspn Dijon mustard
150ml (5fl.oz.) single cream
finely chopped parsley
watercress - for garnish

- Trim the fillet steaks of any fat or skin, and leave at room temperature for ½ an hour to 'relax'.
- Pre-heat a frying pan, turn up the heat, drop in 15g butter and when foaming add the steaks. Sear, turning once or twice, until cooked to taste.
- Blue — on a very high heat - as soon as seared and hot
- Rare — 4-5 minutes
- Medium— 7-10 minutes turning the heat down slightly for the last 4 minutes.
- Well done — 4-5 minutes searing and then place on a preheated dish in a preheated oven 200C. for 10 minutes. (this cooks the steak through without overcooking the outside.)
- Cook the steaks, other than well done ones, at the last minute as keeping them warm, continues the cooking and causes the juices to run.

For the sauce: melt the remaining butter, add the spring onions and cook slightly. Stir in the whisky, followed by the cream and the mustard - the mustard will thicken the sauce. When bubbling add the parsley and freshly ground black pepper.

- Serve the steaks on warm plates, surrounded by the sauce and garnished with watercress.
- Serve extra mustard separately - Arran, Dijon, English.

Château Potatoes

> 500g (1lb.) new potatoes
> (a salad variety is good for these)
> 25 g (1oz) butter
> Seasoning
> parsley

- Wash and dry the potatoes
- Melt the butter and when bubbling add the potatoes. Cover the pan and shake well to coat the potatoes with butter. Cook over a gentle heat, for 10 minutes, shaking the pan from time to time. Remove the lid and fry gently, until the potatoes are cooked. They can be finished in the oven for convenience.
- Sprinkle with salt and pepper and fresh parsley and serve.

Mixed Salad

I always think that steaks and salad were made for each other!

> A selection of salad leaves — Lollo Rosso, Cos, young spinach leaves, rocket, endive , radiccio etc.
> cherry tomatoes
> baby beetroot
> spring onions
> cucumber
> red and yellow peppers
> avocado

- Cook the beetroot until tender, cool and peel.
- Wash all the vegetables and salad leaves and dry well. A salad dryer is very useful and efficient at drying leaves.
- Mix the salad leaves in a large bowl, Add the tomatoes and mix in lightly. Arrange the cucumber slices around the edge. Arrange the beetroot in an overlapping circle. Chop the onions and the peppers and sprinkle over the salad .
- Cover with a damp tea towel until ready to serve.
- Just before serving, slice the avocado and use to garnish the centre of the salad.
- Serve French dressing separately - see page 92.

Baked Autumn Bliss Raspberry Creams

The variety Autumn Bliss enables us to have fresh raspberries right up to November. They are grown on stems produced that year, then pruned to the ground in December or January.

> 250g (9oz) raspberries
> 2 large egg yolks
> 1 large egg
> 60g (2oz) sugar
> 300ml (10 fl.oz.) double cream or crème fraiche
> 250g (9oz) raspberries for garnish
> borage flowers
> icing sugar

- Blend and sieve 250g raspberries.
- Beat the egg yolks, whole egg and sugar to a thick cream, then beat in the raspberry puree, followed by the cream.
- Pour into ramekin dishes and bake in a bain marie for 30 - 40 minutes in a preheated oven 160C.
- The creams will brown slightly and rise like a soufflé.
- Remove from the oven and the bain marie. As they cool , they will sink.
- Chill well.
- To finish, fill the centres with more fresh raspberries and strawberries, sprinkle with icing sugar, garnish with raspberries and borage flowers around the edge of the plate.

Trinity Hill Red (Syrah/Merlot/Cabernet), Hawkes Bay, New Zealand:

My favourite wine on our wine list, this will enhance the steaks perfectly.

'Stylish, full-flavoured red from John Hancock at Trinity Hill. In just 5 short years, this go ahead winery has forged a solid reputation for quality based on fruit from its own vineyards in the famous Gimlett Road area of Hawkes Bay, North Island. The first vintages of the outstanding Trinity Hill Red show just how close New Zealand can come to Gallic finesse - at a somewhat less than Gallic price!'

October

Autumn in the garden

(Watercolour)
Susan Crosthwaite

Menu:

Garden Herb Crêpes filled with
Dunsyre Blue Cheese served with
fresh Tomato Sauce
Monkfish tails wrapped in smoked streaky bacon,
with garlic, thyme, and lime
Smoked Salmon Risotto
Ribbon Courgettes
Cosses apple and blackberry crumble
with Crème Anglaise

October

The colours in South West Scotland in the Autumn are as magical as in the spring. So many of the azaleas, acers and beech trees, to name but a few, are full of colour in the gardens, castles and countryside. Walks around Cosses and the surrounding countryside, reveal woodlands full of Autumn colour.

Sections of the Southern Upland way are suitable for the less experienced walker from Portpatrick to New Luce, passing through Castle Kennedy 37kms/23 miles; and from Bargrennan to Loch Trool 12km /7½ miles. Part of this walk is along the shores of Loch Trool where Robert the Bruce and his men routed the English in 1307. The Galloway and Carrick Forest parks have numerous marked walks catering for a wide range of ability.

The Stinchar Falls - 6 miles - is a superb trail to take on a windy day or, after heavy rain, when one can really appreciate the relative shelter of the trees and numerous waterfalls downstream from Stinchar Bridge. There is a marvellous view of the Stinchar Valley accessed by the Aqueduct road which when backtracked, leads to the largest waterfall with its over viewing platform.

Nearly 20 paths have been joined to form circular routes through the picturesque and historic village of Straiton. The walks take you by riverside, woodland and on to the open hill. Lady Hunter Blair's Walk (2¼ miles) follows the path past the Fowler's Croft Development and Largs Farm, the former home of the covenanter Thomas McHaiffie who was shot after a brief trial by the dragoons, while attempting to escape in 1686. A memorial stands by the west door of the church:

> 'Tho' I was sick and like to die
> Yet bloody Bruce did murder me
> Because I adhered in my station
> To our Covenanted Reformation'

Bruce was the name of the dragoon who had him executed. In the Lambdoughty Glen stands a marvellous variety of trees - hardwoods, conifers with wonderful Autumn colour. The largest waterfall is known as Rossetti Linn after the celebrated poet and painter - Danté Gabriel Rossetti (1828-82) .

The conservation village of Barr is another starting point for a number of circular walks. The Devil's Trail (4 miles) follows the Water of Gregg then climbs through the woods opening out to views of the Stinchar Valley. The walk descends steeply down a gully and across Changue Burn where primroses, bluebells and wild flowers grow. Legend has it that near High Changue there is a site of a famous battle between the Laird of Changue and the Devil. Changue was short of money so he did a deal with the Devil, and sold his soul in return for great wealth. The Laird's fortunes changed and he prospered for many years. When the time came to deliver his soul the Laird reneged and refused to go; placing a Bible on the turf and drawing a circle with his sword around himself. He successfully defied his opponent! The story must be true because to this day you can still see the Devil's footprints, the circle and the mark of the bible visible on the grass. As you descend westwards, the walk back is delightful, with glorious views across the valley.

Closer to home Girvan provides some lovely walks: The Pinmore walk is challenging and full of interest - 11 miles/17km . Follow the track between Sundown valley and Dow Hill. The hill and moorland route branches off to Dalfask Farm and Pinmore. The route passes close to Dinvin Motte reputed to be the finest prehistoric fort in Ayrshire. It is situated on a dominating ridge just north of Pinmore, and consists of a central mound defended by two well defined ramparts and ditches. Just below Dinvin is the 496 metres long railway tunnel built in 1877. The route now follows the quiet valley of Lendal. On a rough moorland track the route skirts the Grey Hills, a wildlife reserve managed by the Scottish Wildlife Trust where patches of herb rich turf can be seen on outcrops of Surpentine rock. From the path you look down on Loch Lochton where white and yellow water-lillies grow. There are magnificent views over the surrounding countryside, the Firth of Clyde, Ailsa Craig, Arran, the Mull of Kintyre and Ireland.

Just north of Ballantrae is Bennane Head, from where you can take the steep cliff path down to the cove where Sawney Bean's cave is hidden. According to legend, Sawney Bean was born in Edinburgh and moved to the remote area of Ballantrae to practice his trade in cannibalism. There was a good supply of passing traffic to and from Ireland and Whithorn , and many travellers would go missing as they passed over Bennane Head. Sawney Bean had a large family - 46 in all - who lived in the caves beneath Bennane Head and would come up to the road and ambush travellers , kill them and eat their bodies. Legend has it that James V1 finally hunted down the family with the help of 400 men and dogs, ambushing them from the sea. They were taken to Edinburgh where they were barbarously executed . The women by burning and the men by having their feet and hands cut off and being left to bleed to death. The determined and the brave can still enter the cave — a torch being an essential accompaniment.

From Cosses itself there are lots of solitary walks where the only likely encounters are with the deer or red squirrels busily collecting their winter supplies of beech nuts and acorns. Wander through the woods, up on to the hills, along the valleys, and pause on the old Ballantrae bridge over the River Stinchar, where you can watch the salmon leap. The small friendly village of Ballantrae, contains the ruins of the mediaeval castle, Ardstinchar (the Bargany Kennedy stronghold), where Mary Queen of Scots stayed and dined on the local delicacy of heron, whilst on a pilgrimage to Whithorn.

The Ballantrae Kirk was created in 1617 and is still the hub of the village; whilst the village hall, opened in 1927, is one of the busiest in the country. Ballantrae was the very heart of the smuggling trade with ships landing contraband, brandy, tea, tobacco and salt , from France via Ireland and the Isle of Man which were carried off through unfrequented paths to Edinburgh and Glasgow. Many secret holes and hiding places existed - even the Kirk was not exempt as it appears the ruling elder masterminded an extensive smuggling body. (Currarie Port, a hidden cove ,just south of Ballantrae - another good walk from Cosses - still has ancient metal rings in the cliff side where the smugglers used to tie up the boats. This steep trail past Kilantringan Loch, where wild goats still roam, was probably used to transport their goods away.)

Along the shore in Ballantrae and past the old fisherman's cottages and the harbour you can walk for 2 miles along the beach to Bennane Head.

South of Ballantrae is one of the most beautiful valleys in Scotland - Glen App
Cosses was part of the Glen App estate when the 3rd Earl of Inchcape allowed many of the farmers to buy their tenancies.

Glen App Church was erected by a Mrs Caddell who bought a portion of the Ardstinchar Estate. She resided at Carlock house, and, as a very forward thinking lady of her time, she built the church to help correct the lawlessness of the 'Glen' people! In 1819, she 'mortified' a sum of money to found and endow the church and a school for the benefit of the tenants of the 'Glen'. This was supplemented by her last will in 1828. Glen App church was not finished until 1849 but the school and the church were a great asset to the valley and its people. The Earl of Orkney acquired the estate followed by Mr James Hunter who had the magnificent baronial castle built from designs by Mr David Bryce, R.S.A. on a sight unsurpassed, in its prospect of land and sea. In 1917 Glen App came into the possession of Lord Inchcape, James Mackay, the great business man who started life as a clerk and became an Earl - the first of Glen App.

The Earl of Inchcape began life in Arbroath the son of a Sea Captain who owned two ships. His father was drowned when one of the ships rolled and he was thrown overboard. As his mother died the same year, 1864, he was orphaned at the age of 12. He had already experienced the sea and said ' If the cook had not grabbed me by the scruff of the neck as I came up for the third time I should have missed a long and delightful life.'

The young James Mackay worked as a clerk in Arbroath and London before going to India where his business acumen was so great that he was made a partner of the firm at 27. No one of his generation held so many directorships or served on more Government commissions. In shipping he was chairman of the P. and O. and British India Steam Navigation companies controlling some 300 vessels. He was vice chairman of the Suez Canal Company, a director of the Great Western Railway, and the National Provincial Bank . Knighthoods of several orders preceded the barony which eventually became an earldom (1929) - but he never forgot that he was born in Arbroath , or, that there he found his wife, Jean Paterson. Jean was the daughter of James Shanks of Rosely, and there followed a long and happy marriage of almost 50 years, with a family of one son and three daughters. The greatest tragedy in their lives occurred in March 1928, when their third daughter, the Hon. Elsie Mackay, lost her life in an attempt to fly the Atlantic with Captain Hinchcliffe. Married to one of the Wyndhams of theatrical fame, she was an accomplished actress, known as Poppy Wyndham and much beloved by the people of the district. As a memorial to their daughter, Lord and Lady Inchcape presented the state with £500,000 which represented the intrepid air woman's fortune stipulating that it was to form a trust to be known as the Elsie Mackay Fund, left to accumulate at compound interest, for 50 years, and then applied to the reduction of the National Debt. Glenapp Church was renovated by the Earl and Countess of Inchcape in memory of their daughter and three stained glass lancet windows were inserted in the east gable to form a memorial. Stained glass windows in the west gable and further renovations were completed as a memorial to the Earl of Inchcape on his death.

He was always deeply interested in the welfare of the village of Ballantrae, and liberally helped with the erection of the village hall and made many improvements to the Glenapp Estate. His estate houses were models and he did much to develop dairying and afforestation. Two new wings were added to the castle, along with other extensions, and the terraced gardens formed one of the most delightful features in the grounds. Above the walled garden is the rock garden which was the special pride of Lady Inchcape. The pond at Cosses and at Auchairne were formed at the same time as the one at Glenapp, probably to be used for curling in the winter as they have special sluices to control the level of water.

The Earl was succeeded by his son, grandson and now great-grandson - the 4th Earl, who continues the Inchcape tradition of looking after its long serving employees for life. The family's main residence is now at Carlock House as the castle was sold to Americans in 1982, and then again to Japanese in 1987 when it was allowed to fall into disrepair. The MacMillan family (of the hotel group in Galloway) moved into the castle in 1994 and have restored both the castle and the grounds to their former glory, transforming it into a very exclusive and luxurious hotel. Glenapp church is often used for the wedding ceremonies for the castle's guests.

Due to our local temperate climate, the vegetable garden continues to supply us with the last of the summer vegetables, and winter brassicas , leeks, parsnips and swedes become plentiful. Winter brassicas often need to be protected from wood pigeons. Leaves need to be swept away and bulbs planted in the containers now that the summer bedding is finished. Asters, schitzostylis and narines create colour in the perennial borders in the Autumn sunshine.

Garden Herb Crepes

300ml (½pt.) milk
2 large eggs
115g (4oz) plain flour
salt and pepper
2 tblspn sunflower oil
a handful of fresh herbs - chives, basil, parsley,
rosemary, oregano, etc.

- Place the milk, eggs and flour in a blender for 30 seconds
- Add the seasoning , chopped fresh herbs and sunflower oil. Blend for a further 30 seconds. Leave to rest for ½ an hour.

Meanwhile make the tomato sauce.

Tomatoes are very plentiful at this time of year and tomato sauce which freezes well is a good way to preserve them.

1 kilo (2lb) tomatoes
3 cloves of garlic
1 large onion
1 tspn dried basil
freshly ground black pepper
3 tblspn olive oil
salt, pinch of sugar,
fresh basil to finish

- Heat the olive oil in a pan and add the finely chopped garlic and onions. Cover the pan and sweat slightly. Roughly chop the tomatoes and add to the onion mixture with all the other ingredients, except the fresh basil.
- Stir well and simmer gently without the lid for 30 minutes,
- Blend and sieve. Reheat when ready to serve.

To cook the Crepes:

- Heat 2 pancake pans - small frying pans which are only used for crepes and omelettes, wiped out with a little salt and kitchen roll, and not washed.
- Brush with oil and add a scoop of pancake mixture, (this should sizzle and start to cook on contact with the pan) and swish around the bottom of the pan.
- As the crepe sets and bubbles , turn over with a palate knife. Leave for 30 seconds and turn out onto a plate. • Repeat, piling up the crepes. Makes 16 - 18.
- Wrap in a clean tea-towel until required.

To finish the crepes:

2 egg whites
85g (3oz) Dunsyre blue cheese   -} enough to fill 8 crepes
freshly ground black pepper

- Beat the egg whites until stiff. Crumble the blue cheese and add to the egg whites, continuing beating until just mixed. Fold in lots of freshly ground black pepper. Lay out 2 crepes per person and divide the cheese mixture between the crepes - about a tablespoon each. Fold over to form a triangle , and fold over the top. Place fold side

down, in pairs, on a baking sheet lined with baking parchment . Bake in preheated oven 200C. for 7 minutes.
- Place tomato sauce around the edge of warm plates, serve 2 crepes in the centre, garnished with fresh basil leaves

Fresh basil grows very well on a warm draught free window ledge. Grow from seed yourself, or buy a pot from the supermarket. Keep using the top leaves, and feed the plant when you water it (only during daylight hours); and it will reward you with fresh leaves for months.

Monkfish Tails wrapped in Scottish Smoked Streaky Bacon with garlic, thyme and lime, and a light cream sauce

550g (1lb 4oz) monkfish tail fillets
8 slices of Scottish smoked streaky bacon
2 cloves garlic - finely chopped
fresh thyme
1 fresh lime
225mls (8fl.oz.) double cream
50 ml (2fl.oz) dry white wine
freshly ground black pepper

Monkfish Tails (sometimes called poor man's lobster), have a lovely meaty texture, without any bones (see April - page 30 for preparation).

- Divide the monkfish into 4 tail shapes. Sprinkle with the juice of half the lime and roll in the fresh thyme leaves and the garlic. Season with the pepper.
- Stretch the bacon with the back of a knife and wrap around the monkfish. Place in a baking dish and pour over the wine. Leave to marinate for about one hour .
- Preheat the oven to 200C. and bake for 10 - 15 minutes, until just cooked. Strain off the juices and keep the fish warm. Add the remaining lime juice to the juices and reduce to 2 tablespoons, add the cream and reheat gently, without boiling - adjust the seasoning if necessary.

Smoked Salmon Risotto

> 175g (6oz) arborio or carnaroli rice
> 1 shallot
> 1 tblspn sunflower oil
> 15g butter
> pinch of saffron threads
> ½ glass of white wine
> 600ml (1pt.) hot chicken or
> vegetable stock - see page 91
> juice of ½ lemon
> freshly ground black pepper
> 55g (2oz) smoked salmon bits
> freshly chopped parsley

- Heat the butter and oil and add the finely chopped shallot. Cook gently , add the rice and stir well for 1 minute, Add the wine and continue cooking until the wine has been absorbed. Add the saffron threads, then gradually add the hot stock a little at a time, cooking and stirring until it is absorbed by the rice, before adding more. Repeat the process until the rice is cooked and the stock absorbed - about 15 minutes. Add the lemon juice, pepper, smoked salmon and parsley. Turn off the heat, cover with a lid and leave to stand for a couple of minutes.
- To serve: fill warmed vegetable rings with the risotto mixture, on warm plates. Arrange the monkfish tails (sliced diagonally) around the rice. Serve some of the sauce over the fish and garnish with fresh parsley thyme and ribbon courgettes.

Ribbon Courgettes

- Top and tail courgettes. Use a wide potato peeler, or mandolin grater to make vertical thin strands of courgettes. Place in a pan with butter or olive oil and seasoning. Over a high heat , stir fry for 2-3 minutes.

Apple and blackberry Crumble with Crème Anglaise

We grow a selection of apples in the orchard at Cosses, Bramleys, Reverend Greaves, and Charles Ross - for cooking. Brambles grow in the hedgerows. They are picked on our dog walking expeditions and Mum and Dad have beautiful ones growing all around their garden which they pick, clean and open freeze for me.

> 500g (1lb) cooking apples
> 250g (½lb) brambles
> sugar to taste
> juice of ½ lemon
> 55g (2oz) organic oats
> 55g (2oz) demerara sugar
> 55g (2oz) SR flour
> 55g (2oz) butter cut into 1 cm dice
> a handful of pinhead oatmeal

- Peel, core and slice the apples into a baking dish. Sprinkle with lemon juice and mix with sugar to taste. I prefer the fruit to be sharp to contrast to the crumble. Gently fold in the brambles.
- Place all the dry ingredients in a mixing bowl and rub together with finger tips or a K beater, until the bread crumb texture begins to come together. Lightly spread over the fruit.
- Bake in a pre-set oven 190C for about 30 minutes until golden.
- Serve with Sauce Anglais.

Sauce Anglaise

> 300ml (½pt.) milk
> 300ml (½pt.) double cream
> 85g (3oz) sugar
> 5 egg yolks
> 1 vanilla pod

- Split the vanilla pod and place in the pan with the milk and the cream. Infuse by heating slowly to boiling point, remove from the heat and leave for 5 minutes. Scrape the seeds from the vanilla pod into the milk and cream, discard the pod.
- Beat the egg yolks and sugar together until thick and pale in colour.
- Slowly add the infused milk/cream.
- Return the mixture to the pan and stir over a gentle heat until the custard thickens. It will coat the back of a spoon and most of the bubbles will have disappeared (aprox 82 degrees centigrade). DO NOT BOIL or the custard will curdle. Should this happen pass the custard through a sieve.
- Serve warm or chilled.

Sauvignon Blanc, Selaks Estate, Marlborough, New Zealand is another great wine to complement this months menu:

'Founded by Croation immigrant Marino Selak, this family-run estate has been making top- notch wines since 1934. This is their signature wine: a big, bold, aromatic style whose luscious fruit epitomises all that's best in Kiwi Sauvignon. Star wine maker, Darryl Woolley, has been associated with Selaks for some 15 years, bringing a wealth of experience from previous stints at Cloudy Bay and other prestigious wineries in both Australia and New Zealand'.

November

Sunset
(Watercolour)
Susan Crosthwaite

Menu:

*Filo Baskets with Courgettes, Peppers, and Leeks
Mornay, surrounded by Fresh Tomato
and Pimento Sauce
Pork Fillet stuffed with Garlic and Fresh Herbs,
with an Apple, Arran Mustard Cream Sauce
Potato and Mushroom Stacks
Steamed Romanesco, Cauliflower, and Broccoli
Hot Chocolate Soufflé*

Ποvember

Magnificent atmospheric sunsets have undoubtedly been a feature of this area since the earliest recorded settlers of 8000 BC. Galloway, at that time extended from the Firth of Clyde to the Solway incorporating Renfrew, Ayrshire, Dumfries and Galloway and parts of Lanark, forming an excellent base for European Stone Age Tribes following the receding ice sheets. This small Pictish Kingdom produced the intrepid explorers who crossed the sea to Ireland, thus populating the Emerald Isle for the first time.

These settlers were followed by Bronze and Iron Age Celtic peoples who left 'Standing Stanes', impressive chambered cairns and enigmatic stone circles as memorials to their dead. These are evident throughout Southwest Scotland - as mentioned in the last chapter at Kilkerran and Dalquharran. Also the finest of all Ayrshire prehistoric forts is to be found at Dinvin, just south of Girvan, - a Pictish fort-hill, described by R.W. Cochran as a perfect specimen of prehistoric hill-forts. Other outstanding examples are at Cairnholy - high above Wigtown and at Torhousekie - between Wigtown and Kirkowan . The similarity of these Neolithic and Bronze Age monuments to others in Ulster is a reminder of the close links with Ireland due to the narrow stretch of water (only 20 miles) for their flimsy boats to negotiate. Remains of frail crafts - hollowed out tree trunk canoes - have been found on both sides of the Irish Channel. Such names as Ballantrae, Carrick and Shalloch appear in both places.

Although marching camps were established at Gatehouse of Fleet and Girvan, in the 1st century AD, the Romans never conquered Galloway, nor penetrated its interior. Traders, at heart, they concentrated instead on retailing along the coastline. This however, was enough to intimidate the Iron Age warriors who built cranogs (fortified settlements on islands in the middle of lochs), and substantial hill forts. They are still seen today at Carlingwark Loch at Castle Douglas, and Milton Loch near Crocketford.

Inspired by the teachings of St. Ninian, the roots of Scottish Christianity lie in ancient Galloway. Known as the British Christian prince, St. Ninian studied and was ordained a bishop in Rome under the tutelage of St. Martin of Tours. For this reason he dedicated the church ('Candida Casa') at Whithorn to Martin's honour. Even now the Roman Catholic church bears the name of both saints. St. Ninian is credited with having converted the Southern Picts to Christianity, and spread his 'Lampas Mundi Luminosa' (the world's bright lamp) across much of Northern Britain. After his death, his tomb became a place of pilgrimage and miraculous healing. Robert the Bruce, James VI and Mary Queen of Scots were among many of the pilgrims passing through Ballantrae on their way to Whithorn. At Whithorn today you can share in the archaeological research investigating the site of the abandoned town. 1000 years ago it was called 'Hwiterne' by the Anglo Saxons. The site of the Northumbrian Monastery is the present level of excavation, with it's timber church. The crypts below St. Ninian's shrine and part of the cathedral have survived, and early Christian sculptures are housed at Whithorn.

There is no authentic evidence to show that the Picts of Galloway were ever ruled by Romans, Norse, Irish, Northumbrians (Anglo-Saxons), English or Scots; even though they invaded Galloway. The area remained unconquered till it was annexed to the crown as late as 1455.

Fergus Mac dubh Gael meaning Fergus of the Clan of the Black Gaels or Picts (1096-1163) was the greatest Lord of Galloway. The Picts of Galloway supported the Scottish King David 1st at the battle of the Standard in 1138. Uchtred and Gilbert MacDowall, sons of Fergus Mac dubh Ghael, invaded England with William the Lion in 1173. Until A D 1186 Carrick formed the north western area of the independent Lordship of Galloway. In that year Galloway was divided between Roland (son of Uchtred) and Duncan (son of Gilbert), by the King of Scotland , William the Lion. He 'confirmed' Duncan as Lord of Carrick and Roland as Lord of the remainder of Galloway. During the reign of Edward 1 of England, the Southern Gallovidians supported their senior kinsman the Balliols and Comyns descendants of Roland); whist the northern, or Carrick, Gallovidians supported their kinsman, Robert the Bruce, (descendants of Duncan). Bruce, with lands near London, Yorkshire, Annandale and Carrick alternated between swearing allegiance to Edward, and opposing him. He deserted William Wallace in 1304; however (after Wallace's execution), all the Gallovidians, of north and south, rallied around Bruce, and at the battle of the Steps o' Trool, in 1307, approximately 1,500 men on the precipitous slopes of Glen Trool and Mulldonach, routed the English. A granite boulder monument commemorate this important victory at Glen Trool and at the east end of Loch Clatteringshaws:

'In loyal remembrance
of
ROBERT THE BRUCE
King of Scots
whose victory in this glen
over an English Force in
March 1307 opened the
campaign of independence
which he brought to a
decisive close at Bannockburn
on 24th June, 1314.

The Red Comyn was stabbed by Bruce in 1306; his daughter married Archibald, the tenth Lord of the Black Douglases. His descendant, James, the 9th Earl of Douglas and 8th Douglas Lord of Galloway was outlawed in 1455 and thus the independent Lordship of Galloway was 'forever' annexed to the Crown, by the Scottish Parliament. The passing of the Black Douglases was followed by a new emergence of power in Galloway — that of the Kennedies (see chapters 5 and 7). Fortunately for the Scottish Crown and the rest of Scotland, but unfortunately for Galloway , this great Carrick- Gallovidian Clan (the Kennedies) became rent in twain, and two and a half centuries of feuding began -1380 to 1631.

During the reign of Mary Queen of Scots, the great struggle for religious liberty came to Galloway .

The Gallovidians generally adopted the National Covenant and the Solemn League and Covenant; and the persecution of these Covenanters involved one of the most tragic stories in Scottish history. There is hardly a church yard in the Southwest of Scotland that does not have a memorial to the memory of these men and women who endured death rather than betray the principals which they held so dear. The ancient Kirk in Old Dailly contains tombstones in the memory of James Semple and Thomas McClorgan, martyrs, slain at their own fireside by the dragoons. The struggle between an Episcopalian king determined on autocracy, and a Presbyterian people determined to have none of it, afforded parallel atrocities, only, to the two world wars. Families were divided between and amongst themselves; in the words of Alex. S. Morton on 'Galloway and the Covenanters': 'The country was devoured with fire and sword. The people were hunted and shot down on the moors and mountains like vermin, their bodies refused burial, and even when interred by friends raised again and hung on a gibbet ......Others were imprisoned, fined of all they possessed .... their crops deliberately wasted, their horses, cattle and sheep driven away, their houses burned down and the plenishing destroyed or carried off. Women were outraged and, as well as men, were tortured, mutilated, and banished from the country ....Trade and agriculture were at a standstill and famine was in sight when the dawn broke. Today it is unimaginable that all this was done simply because the people claimed the liberty to read the Bible, and to worship God according to their conscience.......' The Galovidian population was decimated, many were transported to the West Indies and many sought freedom in the New World themselves to escape the persecution. The survivors and their descendants secluded themselves and took many generations to recover.

Filo Baskets with Courgettes, Peppers, and Leeks Mornay, surrounded by fresh Tomato and Pimento sauce:

- Cut sheets of Filo pastry into 16 cm. squares, brush each sheet with olive oil and place 3 sheets on top of each other (turning each sheet 30 degrees) to make a star. Brush the inside of a ramekin with oil, and line with the star, overlapping the sides. Repeat to make as many baskets as required. Bake in a pre-set oven 210C. for 5 minutes. Remove from the oven, carefully lift the Filo basket out of the ramekin and place upside down on baking parchment, on a baking sheet, to cook the underside, bake for a further 2-4 minutes. Cool.

2 tblspn olive oil
1 tspn paprika pepper
125g (4oz) white part of a leek - sliced
125g (4oz) red pepper, chopped
125g (4oz) courgette, chopped
300ml (½ pint) béchamel sauce - see page 91
75g (2½ oz) Tobermory cheddar cheese - grated
freshly grated parmesan cheese

For the Tomato and pimento sauce :

1 onion - chopped
500g (1lb) tomatoes - chopped
1 tin of pimento - chopped
½ tspn dried basil
seasoning
2 tblspn olive oil
fresh basil

- For cooking, I use an inexpensive olive oil, as a lot of it's properties are lost during heating it, but the flavour with tomatoes is superb.
- Heat the olive oil and add the chopped onion. Cook for 2 minutes. Add the tomatoes, pimentos, seasoning and dried basil. Simmer for 20 minutes. Sieve the sauce and reheat gently.
- Meanwhile heat 2 tblspn olive oil in a frying pan, add the paprika pepper followed by the vegetables, and sauté for 5 minutes until just cooked.
- Bring the béchamel sauce to the boil, stirring all the time, add the grated cheddar, and stir until smooth. Remove from the heat.
- Divide the vegetable mixture between the Filo baskets. Top with the béchamel sauce and sprinkle over the parmesan cheese. Place in a preheated oven 200C. for 3-4 minutes. Place in the centre of warm plates, surround by tomato and pimento sauce garnished with snipped fresh basil leaves and whole leaves. Serve.

Pork Fillet stuffed with garlic and fresh herbs, with an apple, Arran mustard, cream sauce:

550g (1lb4oz) pork fillet
2 cloves garlic
bunch of fresh herbs - thyme, sage, parsley and coriander
2 cooking apples
2 shallots
150 ml. (5 fl.oz) chicken stock
1 glass of dry white wine
2 tspns Arran mustard
150ml (5 fl.oz) single cream
50g (2oz) butter
fresh parsley

- Trim the pork fillet of any fat or skin. Finely chop the garlic and mix with the chopped fresh herbs.
- Make a pocket along the side of the pork fillet and evenly spread the garlic and herbs into it .
- Melt half the butter in a saute pan and seal the pork fillet.
- Keep on one side.
- Peel and core the apples. Reserve 4 rings for garnish, and slice the rest of the apples.
- Melt the remaining butter and fry the apple rings, keep on one side. Fry the shallot for 1 minute and then add the chopped apple and stir. Place the pork fillet on top of the apple mixture, pour over the wine and the stock; and place in the pr-heated oven -200C. for 45 minutes.
- Place the apple rings in the oven with the plates 110C to warm.
- Keep the pork fillet warm whilst making the sauce. Add the mustard and cream to the apple mixture and heat gently, stirring whilst reheating.
- Slice the pork diagonally and arrange 3 -4 slices on each plate. Surround with some sauce and garnish with an apple ring and fresh parsley.

Potato and Mushroom Stacks

4 large potatoes
2 shallots
6 large mushrooms
55g (2oz) butter or duck fat
seasoning

- Peel the potatoes and slice into 12 x 3 mm. (⅛ ins.) thick large rounds - use a plain cutter to trim to make even circles. Wash to remove the starch, and dry well. Melt the butter in 2 large frying pans, and gently fry the potato slices until golden and cooked through.
- Slice the mushrooms thinly and finely chop the shallots.
- Remove the potato circles from the frying pans. Add the shallots to one pan and the mushrooms to the other. Stir fry until cooked. On a baking sheet, place 4 potato rounds; place some shallots on each, followed by some mushroom slices. Repeat with another potato round, followed by shallots, followed by mushrooms. Finish with a potato slice.
- Bake in a pre-heated oven for 10 minutes and serve with the pork fillet.
- Serve with steamed Autumn Brassicas

Winter vegetables are plentiful especially brassicas. Romanesco, resembles a cauliflower, but it is lime green with many pinnacles of curd, with a magnificent flavour. It is sown in May and compliments Autumn cauliflower and broccoli.

- Rinse, break into suitable sizes and steam for 4 - 5 minutes.

November in the garden, is a time for tidying up, putting to bed, and pruning. Removing dead vegetation helps to prevent pests and disease from damaging over wintering plants. Digging over the vegetable garden helps drainage in times of heavy rain, and allows the frost to break up the soil.

Apples, of course are still abundant, and are used in this menu to enhance the pork. It is a good time to make apple and tomato chutney, and mincemeat (for Christmas) to help to use up the apples. The rest, are peeled, sliced and lightly cooked, then stored in the freezer for crumbles and tarts etc.

Hot Chocolate Soufflé

3 large egg yolks
4 large egg whites
85g (3oz) sugar
200g (7oz) plain 60% cocoa solid chocolate
butter
icing sugar

- Brush 4 tall ramekin dishes with melted butter and sifted icing sugar to form a lining.
- Melt the chocolate in a bowl over hot water or in the microwave (on defrost).
- Meanwhile beat the egg yolks with half the sugar, until thick.
- Beat in the melted chocolate.
- In a clean bowl beat the egg whites until stiff, then slowly beat in the remaining sugar.
- Beat a little of the egg white mixture into the chocolate mixture to soften, then very carefully cut and fold the remaining egg whites into the chocolate mixture. Carefully divide between the ramekins and bake in a bain marie for 7 minutes in a pre - set oven 210C.
- Sprinkle with icing sugar .
- Serve immediately with creme frais, whipped cream or ice cream and garnish with piped chocolate leaves.

'Poema' Vinas Viejas Garnacha, DO Calatayud, Spain will enhance the flavours in this months menu:

'Calatyud, in north-east Spain, is a relative newcomer to the international wine scene; but a combination of quality fruit, soil and local ambition look certain to make this a more familiar name in the future. 'Poema' is a stunning example of what is currently being achieved with outside help. Made from old Garnacha vines under the watchful eye of Scotland's very own Pamela Geddes, it shows off the juicy-fruity character of this eminently Spanish grape to perfection. Smooth flavours of cherries and raspberries mingle with cinnamon spice in a ripe, easy-drinking mouthful.

DECEMBER

Cosses Wood and Crailoch Burn in Winter

(Watercolour)
Susan Crosthwaite

Menu:

Ballantrae Prawns wrapped in Marrbury Auld Smoked
Salmon in a Horseradish Mayonnaise
with Salad Leaves
Crailoch Pheasant cooked with Bay, Thyme,
Whisky and Cream.
Pommes Dauphinois
Steamed Brussels Sprouts
Spiced Parsnips
Home-made special Bread and Butter Pudding
Scottish Cheese and Home-made Oatcakes

DECEMBER

All the ingredients for a natural Christmas glow surround Cosses at this special time. The winter gales ensure that there is always a newly felled tree or two to be chopped providing the constant reassurance of a lively, fragrant fire. Plentiful supplies of dogwood, laurel and holly are always on hand to deck the halls and accompany the fragile Christmas rose - a favourite centre piece.

It is also a time of reflection and it only seems fitting to finish with an explanation of Galloway's influence on history. From Fergus and Elizabeth Mac Dubh Ghael, Lord of Galloway (1096-1161), descended our Royal family - to be discussed in this chapter; the Clan Kennedy - Chapters 5 and 7; Robert the Bruce - chapter 2; and the Argyll Clans, Macdougall and Macdonald of Clanranald; and the Black Douglases; and Stuart Kings.

Fergus married Elizabeth, daughter of Henry I of England and granddaughter of William the Conqueror which had consequences beyond the wildest imagination of any historian!

Fergus and Elizabeth Mac Dubh Gael's second son, Gilbert, had a son Duncan McDoaull de Carrick (see February); he was succeeded by his son Neil (or Nigel) McDouall, whose daughter and heiress, Marjory McDouall Countess of Carrick, married Robert de Bruce . Their eldest son , Robert the Bruce became king of Scotland 1306-1329. He married, firstly, Isabella and they had a daughter Marjory, who married Walter Stuart (the High Steward of Scotland). The son of Walter Stuart and Marjory Bruce became Robert the II - the first of the Stuart Kings of Scotland. By his first marriage, Robert II's eldest son John, was crowned Robert III. His daughter, Johanna, married Sir John Lyon.

Robert 111 was the direct ancestor of King George VI - Queen Elizabeth II's father.

The grandson of Sir John Lyon and Johanna Stuart, was Patrick, who became (in 1445), the first Lord Glamis, and thus direct ancestors of the late Queen Mother - who was the daughter of the 14th Earl of Strathmore and Kinghorne and the 22nd Lord Glamis.

Their daughter Elizabeth 11 is our Queen today. (see genealogical chart on page 99)

Ballantrae Prawns wrapped in Marbury Auld Smoked Salmon in a piquant Horseradish Mayonnaise with Salad Leaves

The fishing boats out of Girvan, registered BA (Ballantrae) which used to catch herring, now bring in prawns - many destined for the continent. A Ballantrae fisherman supplies me with some of these. They freeze well and are easier cleaned after being in the freezer. The salmon is smoked locally at the Marrbury Smokehouse, by the Marr family, using a secret 'Auld' recipe of smoking over oak whisky barrel shavings with juniper berries, producing smoked foods of a quality rarely seen these days. Marrbury Smokehouse is close to Glen Trool, set in the Galloway Hills, and does smoked delicacies for the elite of the catering industry. Ruby and Vincent Marr have created a business based on tradition, using Vincent's expertise as a salmon smoker and Ruby's experience as a home economist, and welcome you to their shop and restaurant.

> 3 slices of smoked salmon per person
> 6 medium to large prawns per person, peeled and peel by cutting down spinal cord with scissors, peel back the shell with thumbs and remove the black spinal cord.
> 1 whole prawn per person with just black spinal chord removed by peeling back just enough of the shell. Cook in boiling water flavoured with 6 peppercorns, a drop of white wine vinegar and a bay leaf for 2 minutes. Leave to cool in water.
> 150ml. (5fl.oz) mayonnaise (see page 92)
> grated fresh horseradish
> lemon juice
> 1 tblspn single cream

For Garnish:
> 2 slices lemon and 3 slices cucumber per person
> Strawberries or cherry tomatoes
> Lollo rosso lettuce, rocket and dill.

- Make the piquant mayonnaise by adding the cream, horseradish and lemon juice to the mayonnaise.
- Lay 2 cooked prawns with a little piquant mayonnaise on each slice of smoked salmon and roll up. On each plate lay a selection of salad leaves and place the smoked salmon rolls on top.
- Alternate 3 cucumber and 2 lemon slices (with a slit up the middle) to form a twist and garnish plate with this and tomatoes or strawberries.
- Use a whole prawn to garnish.
- Serve tblspn of horseradish mayonnaise at the side and serve with home-made bread (see page 88) and butter.

Pheasants are shot November through January and it is best to hang them for a week depending on the weather.

Mum and I pluck 3 to 4 dozen each winter - sitting chatting, wrapped up warm on a bright winters day outside or in a barn as the little down feathers are difficult to get rid of in the house.

Crailoch burn (a tributary of the River Stinchar) runs through our grounds, its source being at our friend's and neighbours, Robert and Caroline Dalrymple's farm. They rear pheasants and have a private shoot and kindly supply us with all our pheasants. Caroline, a great cook, gave me this recipe some years ago.

Crailoch pheasant cooked with whisky, cream, thyme and bay

> 1 pheasant 900g (about 2lb) serves 2 people
> 1 small onion, sliced
> 1 carrot, sliced
> a handful of fresh thyme
> 6 fresh bay leaves
> Seasoning
> 75 ml (2½ fl.oz) whisky
> 150ml (¼ pt) single cream

For garnish:
> Celery, leeks and carrots.

- Brown pheasant in butter and oil in oven proof dish then set on one side.
- Fry vegetables for a few minutes, add the herbs. Place the pheasant, breast side down, on the vegetables, season and pour over the whisky and cream. Cover with foil and bake in the oven for 1 hour at 200C.
- Remove the pheasant and keep warm.
- Liquidise the sauce and vegetables and pass through a sieve. Reheat gently whilst carving the pheasant breast. Serve with a little of the sauce and fresh thyme. Serve rest of sauce separately.
- The leg meat is good for paté and the rest makes superb stock.
- Garnish with Julienne of leeks, celery and carrots.
- Cut leeks, celery and carrots into thin strips. Reserve some long green leek strips to use to tie into bundles.
- Steam Julienne strips and reserved strips for 4 - 5 minutes.
- Refresh with cold water and tie into bundles.
- Steam for one minute to reheat and serve.

Pommes Dauphinois - serves 4

> 700 - 800 gm (about 1¾lb) potatoes
> 1 garlic clove
> Butter
> 150 ml (¼pt) single cream
> Salt, pepper, nutmeg
> Fresh parsley

- The potatoes must be sliced immediately before cooking, but may be peeled beforehand and kept in cold water.
- Butter an oven proof dish.
- Finely chop the garlic and heat in cream in a pan slowly until boiling.
- Meanwhile slice the potatoes and layer in the dish - seasoning with salt, pepper and nutmeg. Pour over hot cream and garlic. Cover with buttered foil and bake in oven 190C - 200C for 1-1½ hours. Remove the foil for last ten minutes. Garnish with chopped parsley and serve.

Steamed Brussels sprouts

Brussels sprouts are plentiful in the garden and are particularly good at this time of the year.
- Steam the sprouts for 5 minutes or until just tender.

Spiced parsnips

> 450 gm (1lb) parsnips trimmed and quartered lengthways
> 1 tblspn sunflower oil
> 1 tsp. mustard seed
> 2 tsp. cumin seeds
> 1 tsp. paprika
> ¼ tsp. Turmeric

- Toss parsnips in all the above ingredients and roast for 30 minutes.

Cosses special Bread and Butter Pudding

A real pudding just like Mum used to make. This is a refined version but Mum just used to slice up buttered currant tea cakes, add a few sultanas, and pour over Birds instant custard, sprinkle with nutmeg and bake in the oven!!!

My version:

> 12 tblspn fresh white bread crumbs (must be from unsliced white bread or morning rolls or tea cakes, preferably home-made)
> Mixed dried fruit to taste e.g. raisins, sultanas
> Zest of 1 lemon and juice
> 2 apples peeled and finely cubed
> 2 tblspn sherry liqueur e.g. San Emilio, Pedro Ximenez

Soak all the above ingredients together for at least 2 hours.

For the custard:

> 300 ml (½pt) double cream
> 300 ml (½pt) milk
> ½ vanilla pod
> 55g (2oz) sugar
> 5 egg yolks
> Nutmeg
> Butter

- Heat the milk and cream gently with the vanilla pod to infuse. Meanwhile beat the egg yolks and sugar until pale.
- Scrape the vanilla seeds from the pod into the warmed milk and cream and discard the pod.
- Pour into the egg yolk mixture beating gently until well mixed.
- Divide the bread crumbs mixture into 8 well buttered ramekin dishes (or one large soufflé dish). Pour over the creamy egg mixture. Dot with a little butter and sprinkle a little freshly grated nutmeg.
- Place in a bain marie (a bath of hot water) and bake in pre-set oven 160C until set - about 20 minutes for individual ramekins and 45 minutes for large, depending on depth of dish, until the custard is lightly set. Serve with a little extra cream and a twist of lemon or orange to garnish.

Châteauneuf-du-pape, Domaine de la Janasse, Rhone - a lovely wine to marry with this menu:

'Janasse has become an international name since wine guru Robert Parker paid the estate a visit. 'Just about everything that emerges from this domaine is of impeccably high quality', he enthuses in his Wine Buyer's Guide. And it is true. This Châteauneuf displays the deep ruby-purple hue of one of the best Rhone vintages of recent years; a monumental wine whose heady fragrance of brambles, cherries, pepper and spice sets the scene for the lush textures and flavours of the palate. Ideal with red meat and game.'

SCOTTISH CHEESE

Through a window

(Watercolour)
Susan Crosthwaite

Menu:

Scottish Cheese and Homemade Oatcakes

SCOTTISH CHEESE

This chapter is dedicated to our late friend David Taylor.

D avid's formative years in the cheese trade were spent amid the splendour of Harrods food halls. For ten years he scoured the western world to provide the best for the rich, the Royal and the discerning palate. Always a believer in the ancient but simple traditions of the farmhouse, David did much to champion the burgeoning cheese-making industry which abounds in Scotland today.

He set up "The Real Cheese Company" and taught me everything I know about this particular delicacy, the plural of which is 'cheese'. One of David's pet hates was the wrong use of the word "cheeses". Due to the extensive range of Scottish cheese, in keeping with Cosses tradition for supporting local fare, we prefer to serve a Scottish cheese board. The temperate climate provides perfect conditions for dairy farming and the production of milk to make cheese. Many varieties are only available through wholesalers and special delicatessens. Bob MacKenzie has continued David's vision through "The Real Cheese Company of Ayrshire" (now part of Braehead Foods), and supplies us with the very best of Scottish cheese.

Cheese is best kept at the top of the fridge at 3 - 5C wrapped in the same type of wrapping it arrives in i.e. foil if it is foil wrapped, cling if clinged, waxed paper etc. etc. It should be served at room temperature.

The remoteness from the major markets for liquid milk, and the mild, damp climate has made Galloway, for the last two centuries, an ideal cheese-producing area. Galloway had 13 creameries at one time, but now there are just two - at Stranraer and Kirkcudbright. Much of the cheese was made on the home farms, a tradition re-establishing itself and once the occupation of Cosses Farm for the Glenapp estate. During this time 'draft' (residue from the grain used for making the whisky) was fed to the cows; the Aylesbury ducks discovered that they could peek through the boards and got 'tipsy' drinking it!

Lanark Blue — is the famous Scottish mould ripened cheese, sometimes described as Scotland's Roquefort. It is hand made in a farmhouse creamery from unpasturised ewes milk. The sheep graze hillsides a thousand feet above sea level, overlooking the valley of the upper Clyde.

Dunsyre Blue — is from the same source as the Lanark Blue but is made with vegetarian rennet and unpasturised milk from a herd of Ayrshire cows. The cheese is mould-ripened and matured for about three months with a close, creamy texture and delicious piquancy from the blue veins.

Cheese making has been practised in the Upper Clyde Valley for almost 200 years as a way of using excess summer milk. Sir Walter Scott wrote of the blue cheese of these parts: "we have had the pleasure of eating Scotch cheese....as good as Stilton, and better for it."

Isle of Mull — An old family business owned and run by Chris and Jeff Reade, whose farm, Sgriob-ruadh, is the only dairy farm on the Isle of Mull making a totally unpasturised cheddar from its herd of some 100 cows. The islands moist climate means that grass grows vigorously in spring, when the cows go out and most cheese is made. At Sgriob-ruadh (Gaelic meaning "Red furrow" and pronounced Ski-brooah), the cows are predominantly Friesian, but the milking herd includes Ayrshires and Jerseys. Fine cheese cannot be made without the very best milk. As the cows are milked, their milk is taken directly from the milking parlour to the cheese-making vat. This is a freshness denied to the large factory-like cheese-making plants who rely on milk collected by road tanker. By having complete control over its production and care, as Chris and Jeff Reade have, they are able to ensure that the milk gets the respect it deserves. Isle of Mull cheese is spared the effrontery of pasteurisation as Chris and Jeff believe that it is an unnecessarily brutal way of treating milk used for cheese. Far too many of those organisms which have the potential to create individualism and maturity of flavour are indiscriminately sacrificed in the process. They strive to keep their cheese as natural as possible. From time to time blue veins develop in "Isle of Mull" - this is a sign of rich maturity and considered by many as a bonus. The "Isle of Mull" is made in traditional clothbound cylinders. "Tobermory Truckles" are handmade individually moulded with a dark green wax coating. "Tobermory Flavells" are specially selected mature "Isle of Mull" to which has been added either mixed herbs, cracked black peppers, mull mustard or caraway seeds. Also available smoked or with smoked garlic, they are also waxed.

The **Howgate Cheesemakers** produce a family of fine handmade, award winning cheese.

Howgate Scottish Brie — Named after the village of Howgate, near Edinburgh, where the cheese was first made 30 years ago. It was one of the first cheese of this type made commercially in Britain and is now the longest established.

A distinctive edible white rind cheese, traditionally made with pasteurised milk, it develops a rich soft texture and a mild creamy flavour when fully ripened.

Bishop Kennedy — This style of cheese originated in the middle ages in the monasteries of France, but is relatively unknown in Britain. Bishop Kennedy is named after the 15th Century Bishop of St Andrews who founded the United Colleges of St Andrews University, whose niece is immortalised in the annual Kate Kennedy Pageant in St Andrews.

It is a distinctive orange-red crusted cheese which owes much of its character to the malt whisky liquor applied during ripening. It ripens to become smooth, creamy, quite strong-flavoured and exceedingly smelly.

Pentland — A distinctive, white moulded cheese named after the Pentland Hills which overlook the village of Howgate, where the cheese was first made nearly 30 years ago.

Pentland develops a rich soft texture and a mild, full creamy flavour, becoming runny, slick and pungent when fully ripened.

St Andrews — Named after the nearby famous and historic Royal Burgh of St Andrews.
Pliable, mild, creamy and full of flavour with a golden orange rind.

Scottish Pride Creamery Cheddars "The Mull of Kintyre" — This cheese is a minimum of nine months old and has a pleasant nutty aroma. It is said that it owes its rounded taste to the whisky fumes which still hover within the creamery from its days as a malt whisky distillery.

Highland — This is the most mature of the Highlands and Islands range as it is allowed to mature for at least twelve months which gives it a unique lovely soft texture with a mellow smooth flavour and a fine strong aftertaste.

Arran — Arran cheddar is still made by employing traditional cheese-making methods. The cheese is turned by hand in open vats by a workforce of only six. The result is a deliciously mellow medium to mature cheddar with a creamy-soft texture.

Dunlop Dairy Products: Produced at Clerkland Farm near Stewarton from there own cows, sheep and goats.

Bonnet — This is a fairly mild goats cheese made from pasteurised milk, scalded and pressed overnight, then vacuum packed, known as 'The Bonnet Toon'.

Aiket — This is a pasteurised soft brie type cheese made from cows milk.

Dunlop — This is a mild cheddar.

Swinzie — This is a firm, pasteurised, sheep's milk cheese.

Glazert — A brie type, made from goats milk.

(cont'd)

Grimbister — It has been the tradition on the Isle of Orkney for farmer's wives to use surplus milk to craft the mild and fresh farmhouse cheese. Hilda Seator, who learned the craft from her mother, has carried on this tradition for twenty years. Made from the family's herd of Fresian cows, the cheese is crumbly, deliciously fresh tasting and moist with slightly yeasty or fruity aftertastes as it matures.

Isle of Bute — A medium-hard cheddar with a close texture. It is allowed to mature for 5 - 8 months and is made from the milk from 32 producers on the Isle of Bute and 8 from the Cowal Peninsula.

Highland Fine Cheese of Tain — producers of the following selection:

Caboc — An old favourite - Scotland's oldest recorded cheese and the one most people have heard of. A soft double cream cheese wrapped in oatmeal.

Gruth Dhu — A blend of Crowdie and double cream, rolled in pinhead oatmeal and crushed peppercorns.

Crowdie — The ancient soft cheese of Scottish Highland crofters. Best eaten as fresh as possible. It has a slightly lemony taste, is moist, crumbly and slightly grainy.

Gaelic — A soft, full fat cheese containing herbs and garlic - rolled in nuts.

Hamsa — A low fat soft cheese with added double cream, pepper and wild garlic.

Strathdon Blue — The Glen of Strathdon is a beautiful area in the North East of Scotland, famous for it's quality milk This award winning handmade blue veined cheese has a unique distinctive flavour and creamy smooth texture.

Inverloch Cheese Company

Formally situated on the island of Gigha, but now based in Campbletown, Inverloch is a farm-based independent and family run business. It produces a range of cows and goats milk cheese with some added flavourings which are attractive and all are waxed.

They are:

**Drumloch
Inverloch and
Gigha**

Lochaber — a wonderful soft smoky cheese rolled in oatmeal.

Drumkain — This is unpasturised farmhouse cheddar made by Hazel Forsyth in Dalry, Ayrshire.

Cairnsmore — Millaries Farm at Sorby in Galloway produce a selection of firm, sheep's milk cheese: Plain, smoked or with peppercorns.

I always serve the cheese with home-made oatcakes, a selection of cheese biscuits and grapes. Never butter - Dave always said that there was enough fat in the cheese and the butter detracted from the flavour of the cheese.

Oatcakes

115g (4oz) plain flour
115g (4oz) organic oats
115g (4oz) pinhead oatmeal
15g (½oz) baking powder
55g (2oz) butter
salt
135mls (4½fl.oz.) warm water

- Rub the butter into the dry ingredients until they resemble bread crumbs. Add the water to make a stiff dough.
- Roll out on a floured surface and cut into rounds with a pastry cutter.
- Place on a baking sheet lined with baking parchment. Makes approximately 32 oatcakes.
- Bake in pre-set oven 170C for 20 minutes until crisp.
- Cool in a cooling rack and store in an airtight tin.

Breakfast

Shirred Eggs

BREAKFAST

B reakfast means different things to different people. To accommodate this, we leave a breakfast menu in each room to be perused at leisure. However, whether you choose simple fare, or the full Scottish flavour, it is an excellent time for me to give any guidance required for the day ahead.

The breakfast menu consists of...

A selection of orange, grapefruit and apple juice.
Fruit Compote or Stewed Fruit — consisting of...
Gooseberries, rhubarb, plums, redcurrants, blackcurrants and blackberries, all grown at Cosses in abundance. They all freeze well, thus it is very easy to take a handful of each fruit, put it in a pan with a little sugar (to taste) and leave it to defrost over night. Cook on a low heat, bring slowly to the boil, until the juices run and the fruit is just cooked. Serve in a glass bowl with home-made yoghurt served separately.

Home-made Yoghurt

I have a yoghurt maker which keeps the yoghurt at the correct temperature whilst it is maturing.

Measure the number of yoghurt cartons of milk, you wish to make, into a pan. Heat the milk gently until boiling. Leave to cool to blood heat and pour back into the yoghurt containers, leaving the skin of the milk behind. Stir into each container one level teaspoon of marvel type milk powder and one heaped teaspoon of ready made yoghurt (I like to use natural Greek style for my starter yoghurt). Stir well and then put on the lid and place in yoghurt maker for 6-8 hours. Refrigerate, then use as required.

To maintain ongoing yoghurt re make every 7 days or as required.

Porridge

Still a favourite with a lot of people and a very healthy start to the day. Porridge and herrings used to be the staple diet of many Scots. The porridge would be made overnight and leftovers poured into a special drawer. The men of the house would then cut a 'piece' of porridge to take to work for their lunch. Consequently, when a Scot says that he is having his 'piece' ie sandwich, it comes from the days of a piece of porridge.

Porridge should be made with real oatmeal, (I use medium) soaked overnight in milk or water.

> (Per person)
> 1 rounded tablespoon medium oatmeal
> 150mls (5fl.oz) milk
> 150mls (5fl.oz) boiling water
> salt to taste

- Soak the porridge overnight in the milk in the fridge.
- To make- pour into a pan with the boiling water. Add the salt. Cook over a gentle heat stirring until boiling. Switch off the heat and place the lid on the pan. Then stand for five minutes before serving in warm bowls. Serve with milk or cream. Brown sugar, syrup or honey are optional and depend on taste. I like mine with a little cream whilst Robin likes his with brown sugar and lots of cream!

Fresh fruit salad

A perfect start to any day, freshfruit salad clears the palate and supplies us with many of our required daily amount of vitamins and antioxidants.

The fruit salad can be any combination of fruit, exotic or seasonal, and even in the winter wonderful fruit is available from the southern hemisphere.

Wash all fruit well. I mix a combination of any of the fruits listed below. The only juice I ever use is from the fruit itself and I never add sugar.

> Melons - any variety. Cut out a wedge and remove seeds, roughly chop.
> Papaya - like melon. Cut out a wedge and remove seeds, chop.
> Mango - cut half from the oval stone and slice off peel, chop.
> Pineapple - peel, slice, remove core and chop.
> Physalis - remove husk and cut in half.
> Kiwi fruit - peel and slice - more vitamin C than a lemon.
> Oranges / Satsumas / clementines etc. - peel and cut into segments or squeeze out the juice.
> Banana - peel and slice.
> Pears - peel and slice.
> Grapes - halve and remove pips if seeded.
> Peaches - cut out wedges from around the stone.
> Nectarines - cut out wedges from around the stone.
> Strawberries - cut in half if large.
> Raspberries - leave whole and add at the end.
> Apricots - cut into four, remove stone.
> Plums - cut into four, remove stone.

Brightly coloured fruit has more vitamin C and minerals than pale fruit.

Fresh Grapefruit

Lovely pink grapefruit (much sweeter than yellow) are available all year round. Choose heavy fruit with thin skins as these are juicier. Cut in half and segment with a grapefruit knife. Garnish with a black grape or raspberry in the centre.

Kippers

A rich harvest of fish has always been gathered from the river and sea at Ballantrae. The harbour was built in 1850 and the smoking of herrings over oak chippings used to be practised until the 1970's. The Ballantrae Fishing Banks were closed to allow the herring stocks to expand and they are re-opened from time to time to allow fishermen to catch herrings and prawns. BA (Ballantrae) registered boats are still built locally at Nobles Boat Builders Yard in Girvan - it is also a small dry dock where boats can be repaired. Only small fishing vessels (mainly for crabs and lobsters) use Ballantrae today. Most of the kippers I serve are caught in Loch Fyne and locally smoked in Tarbert.

- To cook the kippers place on a baking sheet in a pre heated oven 200C for 5-7 minutes. Serve immediately.

Smoked Haddock

This used to be naturally smoked in Girvan. Sadly there is no longer a fish shop in Girvan so most of the fish landed there goes directly to the wholesale markets, in Troon and onto Europe. Pieroni now supply me with naturally smoked Scottish haddock which has been oak smoked in Aberdeen.

- I place the fillets on a buttered baking sheet, dot the fish with butter and bake 200C for 5 minutes. Delicious served with freshly laid poached eggs.

Kedgeree (for 2)

For those who like fish and rice for breakfast this is a delicious combination with hard boiled eggs.

> 175g (6oz) smoked haddock
> 85g (3oz) rice (arborio - risotto rice)
> 425ml (¾pt) milk and water mixed
> 1 blade mace
> 1oz butter
> 1 onion - small chopped
> pinch of saffron
> 2 hard boiled eggs
> parsley
> lemon juice
> seasoning (nutmeg)

- Boil the eggs for 10 mins.
- Poach the fish gently for 5 mins in milk/water with the blade of mace. Remove the fish and seasonings.
- Melt the butter in a pan, add the chopped onion and soften slightly. Stir in the rice to coat with butter. Add the saffron, then slowly add the hot milk and water stirring. As the liquid is absorbed add more, stirring until all the liquid is absorbed and rice is cooked.
- Meanwhile peel the eggs, chop one, and cut the other into quarters for garnish. Flake the fish.

- Add the lemon juice seasoning, fish, chopped eggs and parsley. Carefully stir the rice mixture and pile into a warm serving dish. Garnish with the remaining quarters of egg and extra parsley.
- Place in the oven for 2 minutes then serve immediately.

Shirred eggs

This is a recipe I invented at the request of American guests. The eggs are baked on top of bacon and /or mushrooms, or smoked haddock with cream

> 1 large ramekin buttered
> 1 or 2 eggs per person
> 85gm (3oz) smoked haddock
> OR 1 rasher of Ayrshire bacon
> 2-3 medium mushrooms
> 1tbspn double cream
> butter
> seasoning
> cheese

- Cook the smoked haddock by baking for 5 minutes with dots of butter, in the oven at 200C.; or grill the bacon and fry the mushrooms.
- Place flaked fish or chopped bacon and mushrooms in a buttered ramekin (pour the butter off the fish for the smoked haddock shirred eggs).
- Carefully break the eggs on top.
- Season, pour over the cream and sprinkle on a little grated cheese .
- Place in a bain marie and bake in a preset oven 190C. for 10-20 mins depending on how well you like your eggs cooked. Quite a hearty breakfast.

The full Scottish Breakfast (not for the faint of heart!!)

Ayrshire bacon is wet cured in Ardrossan and supplied by my butcher, along with Charlies own recipe pork breakfast sausage (90% pork, plus cereal and seasoning).

Lorne sausage is made by slicing a sausage meat loaf. Black pudding - another butchers own recipe - there is much less fat in Scottish black pudding, it is made from pigs blood, oatmeal and spices and is delicious.

Haggis, another of Charlie's recipes and a favourite of ours, sliced from a roll, (like black pudding,) and made from lambs liver, kidneys, oatmeal and spices.

Potato scones

> 225g potatoes
> 55g plain flour
> salt & pepper
> 25g butter

- Cook the potatoes, drain, mash with the butter, then work
- in the sieved flour with the seasoning to make a pliable dough. Chill wrapped in cling film.
- Roll the dough and cut into thin rounds and prick with a fork.
- Cook on a hot girdle, brushed with oil, for 3 mins on each side.
- Serve warm with butter.
- Alternatively store in a fridge until required, then fry lightly on either side. They freeze well.

Fried bread is just what it says. Preferably use good homemade bread sliced, and fry lightly in hot oil or bacon fat so that it is crisp on the outside and still soft in the middle.

Fried mushrooms-left whole if they are small, or halved or quartered, grilled halved tomatoes and baked beans are the breakfast vegetables. Left over new potatoes, lightly fried are an excellent addition.

Local free range eggs - any way you like them to finish off this gastronomic delight. The hens run about freely in the countryside, thus the eggs have so much more flavour. Eggs should be at room temperature to cook.

To boil: Place in a small pan and slowly pour on boiling water to almost cover the eggs, being careful not to pour directly on to the eggs as they will crack. Cook on high for 5 mins for soft, and 10 for hard.

To poach: I use a small non stick frying pan. Heat the pan slightly, pour in boiling water. Break in the eggs, replace on the heat until the egg changes colour slightly, turn off the heat and leave for 4-5 mins.

To fry: Heat the frying pan a little, add the oil, carefully break in the eggs and cook very gently, basting with oil until cooked.

To scramble: Heat the pan to seal. Cool slightly. Break the eggs into a basin. Add a little milk, and beat lightly. Add a knob of butter to the pan - it should sizzle (but not burn). Pour in the eggs and stir gently until just cooked. Season with salt and pepper.

Now put a selection of it all together!! :

- Put the plates to warm in the oven (90C.)
- Start to grill the sausages, add the black pudding and haggis - turning when necessary, place in the oven when cooked.
- Meanwhile fry the potato scones, potatoes and fried bread. Keep warm in the oven.
- Add the bacon and tomatoes to the grill. Place in the oven when cooked.
- Fry the mushrooms.
- Heat the beans.
- Cook the eggs.
- Serve!

Omelette

- Use a pancake or omelette pan.
- Heat to seal.
- Beat the eggs well .
- Add a little butter or oil to the pan (it should sizzle but not burn).
- Pour in the eggs rotating the pan to spread the eggs evenly. Lift the edges with a palette knife to allow the uncooked egg mixture to run underneath. Season with salt and pepper.
- Cook gently until the egg is cooked underneath, but still creamy on top. Turn onto a warm plate.
- Onions, mushrooms, tomatoes and cheese etc. can be used to flavour omelettes. Onions and mushrooms should be sautéed in the butter and oil before adding the eggs. Tomatoes should be peeled and chopped and added after the eggs with cheese.

(cont'd)

Good bread rolls and teacakes are essential to breakfast. Local bakers produce Scottish breakfast rolls which are delivered to the village about 6.30 - 7am every morning. Robin picks these up with the newspapers every morning. A bacon roll is without a doubt his favourite breakfast (after fruit salad)! - except on Sundays when we enjoy 'the full Scottish Breakfast' for brunch!!

Yorkshire teacake is a recipe given to me by a family friend - Irene Butcher. A slightly sweet bun with dried fruit and spices. As well as for breakfast - lovely toasted for tea.

Irene's Teacakes

> 900g (2lb) strong white flour
> 115g (4oz) butter or marg
> 115g (4oz) sugar
> 55g (2oz) currants
> 55g (2oz) sultanas
> 55g (2oz) mixed peel
> 1 egg
> 2 pkts easy cook yeast
> 1 tsp salt
> 1 tsp mixed spice
> ½ tsp cinnamon
> ½ tsp nutmeg
> 425 ml (¾ pt.) milk

- Using a K beaker on the Kenwood:
- Rub the fat into the dry ingredients.
- Warm the milk to blood heat. Beat in the egg.
- Using a dough hook on the Kenwood:
- Slowly add the egg and milk.
- Knead with dough hook for 5-10 mins.
- Turn onto a floured board and knead.
- Divide and shape into 32 teacakes.
- Place on baking sheets lined with baking parchment.
- Cover with teatowel and place in warm place to rise.

I usually place in a warm oven (70C.) for about 45 mins until well risen.
- Remove the teatowels.
- Turn the oven to 200C. and bake until lightly browned (about 10 mins from the oven reaching 200C.).
- Remove from the heat and glaze with sugar syrup. see p.
- Once cooled these freeze well in plastic bags.

Wholemeal Brown Bread

> 450g (1lb) strong wholemeal flour
> 450g (1lb) strong white flour
> 225g (½lb) strong brown flour
> 225g (½lb) granary flour
> 1 tbsp bran
> 1 tbsp wheat germ
> 1 tbsp oats (optional)
> 2 pkts easy cooked dried yeast
> 1 tspn salt (maldon)
> 3 tbsp sunflower oil
> 1 litre (1¾pt) warm water

I like the combination of flours, rather than using all wholemeal, as it makes a lighter bread.

- Mix together all the dry ingredients. Using the dough hook on the Kenwood, slowly add the oil mixed with the water.
- Knead with the dough hook for 5 - 10 mins.
- Turn out onto a floured board and knead well.
- Divide into four 2lb loaf tins.
- Cover with a teatowel and place in a warm place to rise (e.g.. a warm oven 70C.)for 45 mins plus until well risen.
- Remove the teatowel. Turn up the oven to 200C and bake for 30mins.
- Cool on cooling rack.
- The bread freezes well. (Cut the loaves in half and then you can have it fresh every day).

White Soft grain Bread Rolls

350g (¾lb) strong white flour
350g (¾lb) strong soft grain flour
1 tspn maldon salt
1 packet easy cook yeast
½ litre (18fl.oz.) warm water
3 tblsp olive oil
finely chopped sun dried tomatoes
OR   chopped olives and rosemary

Follow the method for brown bread.

- To make sun dried tomato rolls - finely chop 3-4 sun dried tomatoes and soak in a little olive oil. Knead into the bread mixture used for rolls, then shape into rolls. Brush with olive oil before leaving to rise.

- Serve all the bread and teacakes with Scottish butter, honey, marmalade and jams.

Honey

Kate Dewar, living in Glenapp keeps bees and provides me with local honey. It is a great source of energy. It is a natural antibiotic, it is said that if you are an asthma sufferer that eating the local honey from where you live will help to relieve the symptoms.

Mum often helps me make the jams and marmalades.

Marmalade (makes about 5 kg)

700g (1½lb) seville oranges
700g (1½lb) of mixed citrus fruit,
    eg. a pink grapefruit, a lemon, a lime, a tangerine
2.5kg (6lb) sugar, granulated
2 litres of water

- Wash the fruit
- Put the fruit in a jam pan with the water and simmer gently for 4-6 hours, until the liquid is reduced by half. This is very important, as too much liquid when you come to finally add the sugar will prevent the setting point from being reached without overcooking the sugar and making 'a toffee' sort of marmalade. Leave to cool, then finely chop the fruit, removing the pips- but reserving them in a small pan, returning the chopped fruit to the liquid in the pan.
- Add 300ml (½pt) of water to the pips and boil for 5 mins. Strain into the pan with the fruit, then bring it all to the boil. Meanwhile , warm the sugar in the oven and add it to the simmering fruit, stirring all the time, until the sugar has dissolved. Turn up the heat and boil for about 10 minutes until setting point is reached. Put 10 - 12 jam jars to warm in the oven. To test for setting point - put a little marmalade on a cold saucer, place in the freezer for a minute, then remove and run your finger over it, if it wrinkles, then setting point has been reached. Pour the hot marmalade into the warm jam jars, put on the lids and seal. When cool label and date.

Jam:

As with marmalade the secret of good jam making is to reduce the fruit (and water) to half, before adding the warm sugar, from that point the method is the same as for marmalade.

Blackcurrant Jam:

2 kilo (4lb 4oz) black currants
2.4 litres (4 pints) water
2 kilo (4lb 4oz) sugar

Gooseberry and Elderflower Jam:

2.25 kilo (4½lb) gooseberries
850ml (1½ pints) water
2.7 kilo (6 lb) sugar
20 elderflower heads tied in a muslin - added to the fruit whilst it is simmering, but removed before adding the sugar.

Plum Jam:

3 kilo (6lb) plums
2 pints water
2.7 kilo sugar (6lb)

- Count in the plums and cool the fruit, after simmering, then using your fingers, count out the stones. Place in a pan with a little water and simmer for 5 minutes. Strain into the jam. Bring the fruit back to the boil before adding the sugar.

Damson Jam:

1½ kilo (3lb) damsons
2½ pts water
2½ lb sugar

As with plums.

Sauces, Stocks
&
Miscellaneous

Béchamel sauce ('mother sauce')

1.2 litres (2pt.) milk
1 small onion
1 carrot
1 stick celery
6 peppercorns
salt
mixed fresh herbs - parsley, thyme, basil, tarragon, oregano, bay, sage, chives etc.
115g (4oz) butter
115g (4oz) plain flour

- Infuse the vegetables and the herbs and seasoning in the milk, by bringing it to the boil, and leaving to cool.
- Melt the butter in a pan, remove from the heat and add the flour; stir well. Cook the roux, stirring over a gentle heat, until the flour is cooked.
- Cool slightly.
- Sieve the milk into a blender, add the roux and blend for 30 seconds. Divide between 4 containers and freeze until ready for use.

To use :- defrost at room temperature, pour into a pan and bring to the boil, stirring all the time to make a smooth binding sauce. If a pouring sauce is required add stock, milk or cream to dilute.

This sauce is called 'mother sauce', as it is the base for a lot of sauces:

Mornay - Cheese Sauce: add grated cheddar cheese and ½ tspn made mustard to the cooked sauce and stir till smooth.

Egg Sauce - Add 2 chopped hard-boiled eggs to the béchamel sauce.

Soubise - Onion Sauce: Add 2 large finely chopped onions sautéed in 25g (1oz) butter and 1tblspn. cream to the béchamel sauce.

Mushroom sauce - lightly sauté mushrooms in butter until cooked, add to the béchamel sauce.

Poulette Sauce - vegetable white sauce: dilute with a little vegetable water, reheat and add a little cream, chopped parsley and lemon juice before pouring over the vegetables.

Mustard Sauce - Add 2 tspn Dijon mustard and 1 tblspn. cream.

Parsley Sauce - Add 1 large handful of finely chopped fresh parsley .

Use béchamel Sauce for Lasagne, flans, soufflés , seafood ramekins, feuilleté etc.

Stock

This can be made with different bones as a base i.e.. fish bones, for fish stock, chicken bones for chicken stock, or just vegetables for vegetable stock.

1 chicken carcass or pheasant carcass or beef bones or lamb bones or fish bones such as salmon, halibut or cod bones.

A selection of vegetables :
onion
carrot
celery
leek
turnip
garlic cloves
cooking oil
6 black peppercorns
salt
3 juniper berries
2 bay leaves

selection of fresh herbs:
parsley
thyme
sag,
oregano
tarragon etc.

- Roughly chop the vegetables and sauté in the oil to soften. Add the bones of your choice, cover with water, add the herbs and seasonings; bring to the boil and simmer for 2 - 3 hours.
- Leave to cool , then strain, chill and freeze in convenient size containers.

Demi Glace Sauce

1.2 litres (2 pints) good stock
2 tblspn. finely chopped onion
2 tblspn. finely chopped carrot
2 tblspn. finely chopped celery
2 tblspn. tomato purée
25g butter
2 tblspn oil
2 heaped tblspn plain flour
1-2 mushrooms
1 bouquet garni

- Melt the butter and the oil and add the finely chopped vegetables and sauté until soft. Add the flour and cook to make a roux. Stir in the tomato purée, and cook slightly. Remove from the heat and slowly add half the stock. Bring to the boil, stirring, add the mushroom and the bouquet garni, and simmer for 40 minutes. Remove any scum to clear the sauce, then add ½ the remaining stock, simmer again for 10 minutes, and repeat with the remaining stock. Cool the sauce and then sieve. Divide into 150ml (¼ pt) containers , mark and freeze until ready for use.

Marinated Vegetable Stock

1 onion -sliced
1 carrot- chopped
1 stick celery - chopped
1 leek - chopped
1 parsnip - chopped
slice of turnip -chopped
½ bulb of garlic
2 tblspn. tomato purée
2 tblspn olive oil
1 bottle of white wine
1 litre (2 pints) water
1 star anise
2 bay leaves
Mixed fresh herbs incl. parsley, tarragon, basil, oregano, thyme etc.

- In the oil sweat all the vegetables.
- Add tomato purée.
- Divide the ½ bulb of garlic into cloves and press each with the side of a knife to release the skin and bruise the clove.
- Add to the vegetables with the water and bring to the boil. Simmer for 10 minutes.
- Add all the herbs and season with maldon salt and whole peppercorns.
- Add the wine and leave to cool.
- Cover and marinate in the fridge for 48 hours.
- Strain and divide into small containers - freeze.
- Defrost as required for use.

Mayonnaise

1 large egg
1 large egg yolk
3 tblspn white wine vinegar
1 heaped teaspoon dry mustard powder
1 teaspoon salt
20 grind freshly ground black pepper
1 teaspoon sugar
75 ml (2½fl.oz) extra virgin olive oil
150 ml (5fl.oz) sunflower oil

- Place the egg and egg yolk in a blender with the white wine vinegar (the vinegar will kill any salmonella - but if the eggs are fresh then there will not be any salmonella bacteria as it takes three weeks for it to mature!)
- Add the mustard , pepper, salt and sugar and blend on high for 30 seconds.
- Whilst the blender is on full , pour a steady stream of oil onto the eggs. It will thicken as the oil is added.
- Pour into jar and store into the fridge.

French Dressing

1 tspn dry mustard powder
1 tspn salt
½ tspn. sugar
20 grinds of black pepper
1 tspn Worcester sauce
2-3 cloves garlic - peeled but left whole (optional)
⅔ olive oil and sunflower oil to ⅓ white wine vinegar (the types of oils and vinegars can be altered to suit one's tastes and recipes).

- Place all the ingredients in a sealed container and shake well until thick.

Sugar Syrup

250g (9oz) sugar
200 ml (7fl.oz.) water
25g (1oz) liquid glucose

- Combine in a pan, bring to the boil and simmer for 3 minutes.
- Cool and store in a container in the fridge.

To make elderflower syrup: add a dozen elderflower heads (washed) to the hot syrup and marinate until cold. Pour through a muslin to sieve.

To make melba sauce:

Add 400 g (14 oz) raspberries to
135 ml (4½ fl.oz) sugar syrup
Juice of half a lemon

- Place in a blender for 30 seconds and then sieve.

Redcurrant Jelly:

3 kilo (6lb 6oz) redcurrants
1.2 litres (2 pints) water
sugar

- Take two extracts from the pulp, using just over ½ the water for the first extract. Blend the two extracts and measure.
- Bring to the boil and add 750g sugar to each litre of juice (1lb sugar to each pint)
- To take the extracts: soften the fruit in a jam pan with ⅔ the amount of water. As soon as the fruit has cooked to a pulp, strain by tipping into a scalded jelly bag, having first placed a wide basin underneath to catch the juices. Leave the pulp to drain for 15 minutes. Return the pulp to the pan with the rest of the water and simmer for 30 minutes , then drain the pulp for several hours, or until no juice is dripping through. Do not squeeze the bag as this will make the jelly cloudy! Mix the two batches of juice , measure, bring back to the boil, add the warmed sugar and boil for 10 minutes before checking for setting (as with marmalade - see page 89).

These are some of Mum's baking recipes, which appear at Cosses on the afternoon tea menu:

Plain Scones

> 225g (8oz) self raising flour
> pinch salt
> 50g (2oz) butter
> 1 egg beaten and made up to 150ml. (¼pt.) with plain yoghurt

For sweet scones add 1 tblspn. sugar; OR for cheese scones add 75g (3oz) strong cheddar cheese and ½ tspn dry mustard; and for fruit scones add 50g (2oz) currants and sultanas.

- Heat the oven 210C.
- Rub the butter into the dry ingredients, to resemble bread crumbs, add optional ingredient if desired, and finally the egg and the yoghurt. Form into a dough and place on a floured board. Flatten with a rolling pin , then fold into 3. Repeat twice more. then roll to the required thickness - 1cm. (½ ins.).
- Cut out with a pastry cutter and place on baking parchment, on a baking sheet. Brush with egg and milk. Bake in pre-set oven for 10 minutes.
- Cool on a rack

Oat Biscuits

A great favourite with our guests, and found on the tea trays in the rooms.

> 115 g (4oz) organic oats
> 115g (4oz) SR flour
> 115g (4oz) sugar
> 115g (4oz) marg
> 1 dessert spoon golden syrup
> 1 tblspn hot water
> 1 level tspn baking soda

- Melt the marg and the syrup in a pan with the water and baking soda. Add to the mixed dry ingredients. Roll into balls and press onto a lined baking sheet , levelling with a fork. Makes about 36. Bake 170C for 10 minutes.

Very tasty ginger cake

350g (12oz) SR flour	175g (6oz) sugar
175g (6oz) marg	3 heaped tspn ground ginger
¾ tspn. bicarb. soda	3 tblspn golden syrup
2 eggs	1 cup of hot milk

- Warm the marg, syrup and the sugar in a pan.
- Mix the flour, ginger, and bicarb. soda together.
- Beat the eggs.
- Heat the milk.
- Add all the above together and mix - it will be a pouring consistency.

This will make 2x1lb loaves or 1 square 14x8x1 ½ inch deep which will cut into squares.
Bake 150C for about 45 minutes - 1 hour.

Chocolate Cake (Liz Taylor's Favourite)

115g (4oz) marg
115g (4oz) sugar
2 large eggs
115g (4oz) SR flour
1 heaped tblspn cocoa
1-2 tblspn milk

- Beat the marg and the sugar together until light, pale and creamy (in a Kenwood with the K beater).
- Beat the eggs and slowly add to the sugar and marg mixture with the Kenwood on full speed. Beat until light and fluffy.
- Sieve the flour and cocoa together and carefully fold into the mixture, adding as much milk as necessary to keep a soft texture.
- Pile into a lined 7 or 8 inch baking tin and bake in a pre - heated oven 170C for about 45 minutes.
- Turn onto a cooling rack.
- When cool, split in half and fill with chocolate butter. cream, and finish by sprinkling with sifted icing sugar.

Chocolate Butter cream

55g icing sugar
1 tspn cocoa
40g (1½oz) unsalted butter
a little boiling water

- Sift the icing sugar and cocoa together and beat in the softened butter and a little hot water to make a soft texture.

Lemon Cake

- Follow the recipe for chocolate cake, substituting the grated rind of a lemon for the cocoa, and the juice of the lemon for the milk.
- Ice the top of the cake with sifted icing sugar mixed with lemon juice.

Vanilla Ice cream

Custard made with egg yolks and cream is the traditional base of many ice creams. This is a classic vanilla ice cream but if the vanilla is omitted many different flavourings such as fruit purées etc., can be added to cold custard. Chocolate (60% cocoa solids) should be added to hot custard to make chocolate ice cream.

4 egg yolks
115g (4oz) sugar
300ml (10fl.oz.) milk
300ml (10fl.oz.) double cream
1 vanilla pod or 1tsp. vanilla extract

- Pour milk and cream into a pan and infuse the vanilla pod (if used). Beat egg yolks with sugar until pale and creamy.
- Remove the vanilla pod and scrape the seeds into the cream. Pour onto the egg yolks. Return to the pan and cook gently until thickened - but do not allow to boil.
- Pour into a bowl and leave to cool. If using vanilla extract add to the cold cream.
- Pour the mixture into an ice cream maker then freeze.
- Remove from the freezer and allow to soften slightly before serving.

still, more than 20 years on, a key supplier for Alexander Wines. He remembers those early days with nostalgic fondness, recalling the nights spent sleeping among the boxes in the back of the transit van 'to save the cost of a hotel.' Mechanical difficulties and a faltering French were another hazard. But Frasers's evident enthusiasm for the region's wines was enough to win over even the sceptical vigneron.

During the 1980s, business in Glasgow grew steadily as restaurants boomed and wine-drinking became more popular. Alexander Wines moved into 'real' premises and rented space in a bonded warehouse. Staff were employed to man the office and deliver the wine expanding into Ayrshire. In the early 1990s, the company moved to Hillington, by the M8 motorway with extended warehousing facilities that made life easier for the rapidly expanding business.

The 1990s witnessed a huge increase in demand for wine which saw Alexander Wines promoted to the forefront of the on-trade in Glasgow. By this time, Fraser was sourcing wines from every corner of the globe - South Africa, Australia, California, Spain, Hungary, Canada...... a total of 14 different countries. Today, this impressive and varied portfolio of over 600 wines includes such famous names as Laurent-Perrier Champagne, Marqués de Riscal Rioja, Pendarves Estate - Hunter Valley, Château Kirwan, Simonsig Estate and Valdespino Sherry as well as a good selection of 'Jewel in the Crown' small 'Boutique' producers. Wherever possible, the wines are shipped direct from the supplier, thereby guaranteeing authenticity, better stock control, price and quality to the final consumer.

G lasgow-based independent Fine Wine merchant Alexander Wines supplies wines from around the world to many of Scotland's best restaurants including Cosses Country House

The company was founded in 1981 by the proprietor, Fraser Alexander. Just 23 at the time, and armed with a degree in Technology and Business Studies, Fraser had developed a passion for wine during a stint as a student in the vineyards of Baden, Germany. While his friends wrote their dissertations on more conventional subjects, Fraser submitted a paper comparing winemaking methods in Baden with those of the neighbouring French region of Alsace...

After graduating, Fraser spent a few months 'sweeping tennis courts and wondering what to do', before landing his first job in the wine trade as regional representative for a wine company. Fraser soon left to start his own business, he took with him some very useful experiences, together with a firm belief in the future of wine drinking in Scotland.

To begin with, he operated as a one-man band from the family home, There was no office and no staff. Undaunted, Fraser set off for the Loire Valley in a ramshackle old transit van, determined to seek out the best suppliers. He struck gold with Domaine Henri Poiron, one of France's best producers of Muscadet and

Culinary trends in Scotland have changed and whether your food requires bold up-front New World wines or delicate restrained wines from the traditional wine producing countries (nowadays they both produce the complete spectrum of styles) there is a wine to complement each dish.

Throughout its two decades of existence, Alexander Wines has remained firmly committed in focus on sourcing quality wines that offer consistent value, that food and wine go hand in hand, they are meant to be enjoyed together.

Block 4
Munro Place
Bonnington Industrial Estate
Kilmarnock
Tel: 01563 550008 Fax: 01563 550038

This independent company supplying the cream of Scotland's hotels and restaurants is unique. Founded by John Peter Houison Craufurd in 1988, Braehead Foods evolved from the estate practice of breeding its own pheasant for the shoot. It was decided to breed in tandem their Craufurdland Guinea Fowl and to deal in Gressingham Duck. From these classic items, a whole variety of specialist food and game has been added, the first class fare that visitors expect from traditional Scotland.

Braehead is now owned by Craig Stevenson, a food specialist with 21 years experience of production, sales, marketing, distribution and quality control and has merged with the Real Cheese Company of Ayrshire.

A team of twenty ensures fast and reliable service with the very latest refrigerated vans and purpose built state-of-the art storage and preparation unit. Hazard-analysis and Critical Control Points System is a method now recognised as the bedrock programme of total safety in food and refrigeration.

Gressingham Duck, a British hybrid duck, bred from Peking and Mallard, is increasingly recognised as top of the market, with its high ratio of meat to bone with a full flavour. Braehead have sole distribution rights in Scotland.

The company takes pride on being quality game suppliers with a complete range of all game, cut and packaged to individual requirements and a range of Scottish cheese surpassed by few.

DALDUFF
Farm Shop
Serving Ayrshire since 1978

The finest and freshest meat straight from the farm

Dalduff Farm Shop was set up in 1978 by Jim & Dorothy McFadzean, and for 25 years they have dedicated their lives to sourcing and producing the very best in Scottish meat.

Prices are available on request and are subject to change, and all products are subject to availability, however as long-established local suppliers of prime Scottish beef, pork and lamb, we endeavour to fill your requirements and expectations as best we can.

We take pride in our skills and experience as master butchers and we are here to cater for your needs. We are happy to give as much advice and information as possible especially with regards to traceability and quality. We have been producing our own range of sausages and pies here on the farm, using only the finest locally produced meats and under strict hygienic conditions, for many years. We do not, and will not, sell any genetically modified produce, nor is it knowingly used in any of our own products.

We operate a full HACCP control system, and we can deliver daily by refrigerated transport. We offer a full back-up service and guarantee for all goods provided. It is our aim to provide complete satisfaction and an honest reliable service.

Dalduff Farm Shop, Crosshill, Maybole, Ayrshire KA19 7PU
Tel: 01655 740271   Fax: 01655 740550
www.dalduff.co.uk

Genealogical Chart

Showing descent from Fergus Mac Dubh Gael (MacDouall)
Lord of Galloway, 1096-1163, of Both branches (King George VI and Elizabeth the Queen Mother) of the reigning family of Britain.

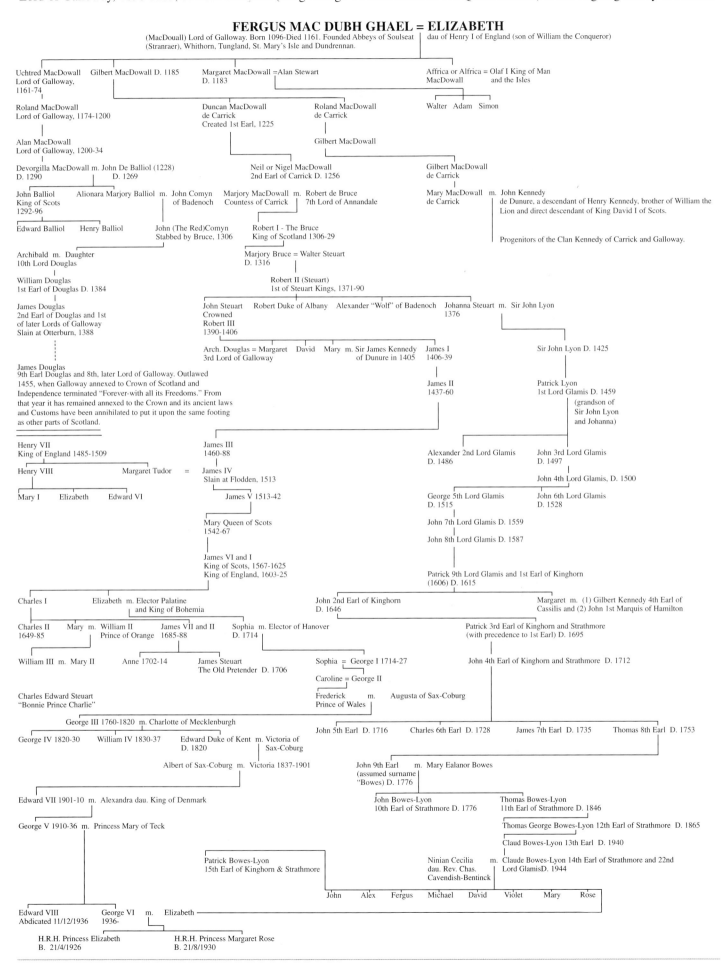

Daffodils at Bargany

(Watercolour)
Susan Crosthwaite